A GENTLE UNFOLDING

Published in 2018 by

David Lovell Publishing
PO Box 44 Kew East
Victoria 3102 Australia
tel/fax +61 3 9859 0000
email publisher@davidlovellpublishing.com

© Copyright 2018 Judith Scully

Apart from any fair dealing for the purposes of private study, research, criticism or review, as permitted under the Copyright Act, no part may be reproduced by any process without written permission. Inquiries should be addressed to the publisher.

Cover image: John Hurl

Design by David Lovell Publishing
Typeset in 11.5/16 Perpetua
Printed in Australia through Ingram Spark

National Library of Australia card number
and ISBN 978 1 86355 168 7

Full Cataloguing-in-Publication details available from
the National Library of Australia

A GENTLE UNFOLDING

CIRCLING AND SPIRALLING INTO MEANING

Judith Scully

David Lovell Publishing
Melbourne Australia

Every year unfolds like a petal
inside all the years that preceded it.
You will feel your thinking springing up
and layering inside your huge mind
a little differently.
Your thinking will befriend you.
Words will befriend you.
You will be given more than
you could ever dream.

Naomi Shihab Nye
A Maze Me: Poems for Girls
HarperCollins New York 2105

Dedication

I walk in the footsteps of the women who came before me:

Great-grandmothers
Maria Warren (1834 – 1917) and
Elizabeth Ann Tonkin (1853 – 1931).

The grandmother I never knew
Elizabeth Maria Gilligan (1876 – 1930).

Florence Anstice Helyar (1887 – 1957)
who left me a memory I call Tarella.

Contents

1. Falling in love	1
2. Cradle Catholic	7
3. Little black dress	13
4. A suitcase of whites	19
5. Mission memories	25
6. 'Here be dragons …'	31
7. Cloud walking	37
8. Motor Mission	42
9. Mothering	48
10. A baby girl	54
11. Ordinary Time	59
12. *Let's Go Together*	64
13. Church lady	70
14. Pastoral associate	75
15. Faith educator	80
16. Ripples	85
17. New beginnings	90
18. Spiritual Director	95
19. Tarella space	100
20. About Terry	106
21. Country lady	113
22. Being church in Australia	119
23. All beginnings have endings	126
24. Once upon a story	132
25. One size fits all	138
26. You can't lose the plot	145

1
Falling in love

At some point in my early teens, just when I was discovering there was more to the opposite sex than beneath-my-notice little brothers, I fell in love with God. Which is why, aged sixteen, wearing a fetching little hat and my first pair of high heels, I left my weeping parents on the Spencer Street railway platform and chuffed off to be a nun.

It was 1954. Pius XII had been Pope for what seemed to be forever and Daniel Mannix had been Archbishop of Melbourne all my life and even before that. Robert Menzies was elected Prime Minister the year I started secondary school and I would be thirty when he finally retired. My mother's sister would proudly tell me that my once-teenage grandmother had occasionally babysat a very young Robert Menzies while his parents were busy in their Jeparit store.

One February morning that year I jostled my way through the cheering crowd lining Mount Alexander Road to get a glimpse of a young Queen Elizabeth, as she and Philip went by on their coronation tour of the empire she had inherited. Australian teenagers were queueing up to buy *The Happy Wanderer* on a 45 rpm disc and pre-schoolers like my youngest brother were those who would be later labelled post-war baby boomers. All in all, it was a good year.

A Gentle Unfolding

Now I ask myself – how did I do it? How did I wave goodbye and leave it all behind?

I was sixteen, had completed my Leaving Certificate, just, and been accepted for teacher training at Mercy Teachers' College. Teaching was a heart choice. Ever since I was a little girl I had wanted to be a teacher, so by entering the convent I wasn't opting out of an unwanted career choice. I loved fashion, and with all my adolescent heart longed to be allowed to wear shorts in summer and a daring strapless dress with a swirly skirt. My mother, a daughter of straight-laced Methodist parents, would have none of it. I wasn't even allowed to wear slacks. But I was prepared to exchange colourful cotton summer dresses and high heels for cover-me-all-up black serge and daggy lace-up shoes.

I was saying goodbye to annual family holidays in the Dandenong Ranges, or sometimes at the beach. We'd rent a house for two weeks and do all the things that families in the 1950s did, because now there was more money for such things. I enjoyed exploring a house that wasn't ours, reading the books left behind by other holiday-makers, waking up to a different landscape.

From my position as the only girl and the eldest, my younger brothers were just about beneath my notice. The age gap was substantial and there were three of them to one of me. Occasionally I would wish that I had a sister, someone who was like me. It wasn't till secondary school that I found a best friend who filled the gap for me. Sadly, I would never see or hear from her again after I entered the convent, as outside friendships were not permitted.

As an only girl, I'd never had to share a bedroom and didn't realise that leaving home would mean leaving behind a room of my own. For the next seventeen years I would sleep in a dormitory, the beds separated by curtains pulled around our few feet of space each evening at bedtime. Sometimes, for reasons of seniority or illness, a sister would

Falling in love

be given a room of her own and I would feel a surge of jealousy mixed with deep longing for a space of my own. Even my name, the name I was given at birth and that identified me as someone who belonged to a particular family, that too would be left behind and I would be known by another.

My relationship with my mother would stall at adolescence and never get a chance to develop into the adult mother and daughter thing that each of us wanted but didn't know how to achieve. She wasn't one to show her feelings and it was only after she died that my father told me that she cried herself to sleep for months after I left home.

I would miss out on all the learning that happens in young adulthood, the years when school friends give way to adult relationships, and boyfriends would be tried out and discarded, like trying on shoes for style as well as comfort. Some of this I knew in a vague kind of way, but the rest would creep up on me during the years that followed. I was in love, and when you are in love you will go wherever and whenever the loved one calls. It reminds me of the story that depicts God as the owner of a vast store that sells all that one could desire, and then more. It's only when the customer takes their choice to the checkout that God rings up the cost. The cost of my years in religious life has followed me down the decades.

My brothers grew up, left school, started work and got girlfriends. I missed two of their weddings and the opportunity to form relationships with the girls they married. I'm the one missing from the family group photos taken on birthdays and other special occasions. Babies were born, and suddenly my parents were being referred to as Nanna and Grandpa. The family home was sold and in the packing up I assume that whatever was still left of my childhood books, dolls, school reports and letters was either misplaced or went to the tip.

A Gentle Unfolding

With one exception, in Grade 5, I was taught by religious women, most of them young, and my all-girl secondary school was staffed solely by nuns – Daughters of Our Lady of the Sacred Heart (OLSH). I was intrigued by their lifestyle, by what the convent might actually look like inside its closed doors. I longed to know what their 'real' names were and where they had gone to school. I wondered what they might have looked like under their voluminous robes and architectural headdresses. Did they wear a bra? I couldn't believe that they got their period every month like me! These women were my role models. I admired them and yearned to emulate their lifestyle, to become a Daughter of Our Lady of the Sacred Heart

Every year the senior students went on retreat, and while some of the girls were bored I relished the unaccustomed silence and permission to sit in the cosy little chapel and dream – of what, I'm not too sure. I was drawn into a peaceful place where I could somehow be myself without actually knowing who that self was. Life was on the cusp of unfolding and I knew God was beckoning.

I began taking myself off to the parish church for Sunday benediction and the weekly novena. Some Sunday afternoons I would cycle up to the church and sit there, not knowing what to do in a space that felt so right, not knowing if there were words that I should be saying –and at the same time knowing that words were useless. On the one hand my mid-teen self was being itself, stretching for the transcendence that comes with leaving childhood behind, confused by feelings looking for somewhere to belong. On the other hand I was falling in love with God.

In the absence of any real discernment or advice to the contrary, I assumed that religious life was the only way to live out the swirl of yearning I felt inside. In Catholic circles it was called having a vocation or 'entering'. In voices filled with awe or surprise – and sometimes

Falling in love

disbelief – the news would be passed around: 'So-and-so is going to enter.'

In the late nineteenth and first half of the twentieth century, it was a matter for pride in Catholic families when one of the children left home to become a sister, priest or brother. Occasionally, such vocations tapped into left-behind parental dreams of religious life or priesthood. Sometimes, too, young women or men chose religious life as a means of escape from poverty, sexual abuse or alcoholic violence. None of the above was true in my case. God had called and I was answering. 'You have seduced me, Lord, and I have let myself be seduced' (Jeremiah 20:7).

Towards the end of Year 11, I told my parents that I had a vocation. Being good Catholics and taking their cue from the nuns, who were delighted with the news, they agreed – but with one stipulation. My mother insisted that before I entered I had to get some kind of experience outside the classroom. So I cancelled my teachers' college application and applied for a job at the local Coles store. I spent the six months between the finish of school and my entrance as a postulant with the Daughters of Our Lady of the Sacred Heart working on the haberdashery counter. I liked earning money and being able to buy a pair of shoes that my mother considered unsuitable. I didn't like standing up all day and the tedium of keeping a counter full of handkerchiefs, elastic and such things neat and tidy.

Now, six decades on, I still try to put logical reasoning around my decision to enter religious life.

Becoming a nun wasn't a mistake but a choice all tied up with the mystery that is God, a tentative, if adolescent, step towards living out my baptismal call, my Christian vocation. Falling in love with God was the easy part; but staying in love – that's adult – and God, who works in and through each individual story, was prepared to wait.

A Gentle Unfolding

I remember almost nothing of my last weeks at home, just my father hugging me minutes before driving me to Spencer Street station. I think he was crying though I couldn't really see, but I remember his words, 'Don't ever be afraid to come home if you need to.' Nearly eighteen years later I did just that.

2
Cradle Catholic

I am what is known as a cradle Catholic, but could just as easily have been a Methodist. My Methodist mother met my Catholic father on the tennis court of a guest house where both were holidaying. A courtship followed and when my mother chose not only to marry this rather shy young man but to become a Catholic she was disowned by her mother. Her mother went further, forbidding the family to attend the wedding, something two of my mother's brothers ignored.

My grandmother was a devout Methodist and took her religion seriously – no drinking, no dancing, no gambling, no Catholics. On the other hand my father's family were what I like to describe as Sunday Catholics. Unlike the Methodist clan he married into, which fairly bristled with deaconesses, missionaries and lay preachers, there were no priests or nuns in the Scully family tree.

I'm grateful there were no hand-me-down family names waiting for me when I was born in 1937, otherwise I might have ended up being named Florence or Gertrude after my mother and her mother. Instead I was named Judith, possibly because it was one of the top names for girls that year. Aged two weeks, I was baptised in St Patrick's cathedral and officially became a Catholic. All the words and

A Gentle Unfolding

wonderful symbols of the baptism liturgy meant nothing to my baby self and I was a long way into adulthood before I began to appreciate that the liturgy surrounding baptism was the closest we can get to a human understanding of God's gift of life, both here and in the hereafter. There's a lot to be said for adult baptism.

My baby charms must have melted my grandmother's Methodist bias towards Catholics, because until I left home for the novitiate I spent part of each summer school holiday with her. Ill health had meant that she was forced to hand over to her sons the land she had farmed since the death of her husband years before and move to the nearby little country town. There she lived with her unmarried daughter. I will always be grateful that it was my early memories of my grandparents' original home, known as Tarella, and its surrounding landscape, that moved me beyond my everyday horizons and into the wide spiritual dimensions of life.

If there is such a thing as a religious gene, then the one that I've inherited would be labelled Christian Methodist. My grandmother prayed every night before she went to sleep and she had a well-thumbed Bible on her bedside table. Meals at her table always began with a formal grace and every Friday my Catholicity was respected with meatless meals. She arranged for a neighbouring Catholic family to take me with them to Mass on Sunday while she and her daughter attended the local Methodist chapel.

She practised a steely kind of religion that emphasised a highly moral lifestyle and fidelity to basic Christian beliefs. Whenever I find myself experiencing, or, worse, voicing a lack of tolerance towards religious practices that lack theological or scriptural foundations, I have one of those 'blood is thicker than water' moments.

Between 1937 and 1949, when the last of my three brothers was born, Australians were involved in World War II and women were

Cradle Catholic

employed in jobs that took them out of the home and into a world that would soon introduce them to feminism. Our population grew from seven million to close to ten million, and Catholics began to be recognised as having a part to play in the Australia that was emerging.

Since the early days of Australia, Catholics had been regarded with suspicion and outright hostility, and were kept out of many mainstream employment opportunities. However, by the end of the 1940s Catholicism in Australia was on a high and new Catholic parishes were being created in the rapidly growing outlying suburbs. There everybody was a new parishioner and the church quickly became the centre of Catholic life.

Friendships, often life-long, were forged around fund raising to build schools and churches. There were tennis clubs and youth clubs, debutante balls and whist evenings. Babies were baptised, went to Catholic schools, joined one of the youth organisations and often went on to marry a good Catholic boy or girl. Unless of course you had a vocation, in which case you become an unpaid teacher in one of the Catholic schools springing up across the country or were ordained, replacing the aging Irish clergy.

Both of my father's parents had Irish ancestry but a couple of generations in Australia seemed to have papered over or discarded the religious practices and family stories that were often passed down in families with a similar background. This might have been different if my father's mother had not died at a relatively young age. Her husband, my grandfather, was a hard, somewhat unfeeling kind of man who had little time for children, his own or others', and never told stories about 'the good old days' in Tasmania, so we have no family stories or traditions. My mother's Methodist background meant that she was unfamiliar with the religious baggage that swirled around the 1940s and 50s under the name of Catholicity.

A Gentle Unfolding

We were an ordinary, if not very pious, Catholic family and we did basic Catholic things. All four children were baptised, made first communion and were confirmed. Sunday Mass was a must, even when we were on holidays in an unfamiliar area. In an era when communion at Mass was only occasional and always preceded by confession, once a month confession followed by communion was the norm. Money was set aside for school fees, known as school money in my primary school days, and collected first thing on Monday morning. Later on all four of us were sent to Catholic secondary schools.

Unlike some Catholic families, we didn't say a meal grace and I don't recall night prayers being enforced. With the exception of an illustrated Irish blessing, the gift of our Irish parish priest at the time, there were no religious pictures or statues in the house. After Father Peyton's Rosary rally in Melbourne, attended by 75,000 people, Mum and Dad made a half-hearted effort to say the family rosary, but we never really stuck to it. Maybe they found the repetition tiresome. I know I did.

We rarely attended devotions such as Sunday night benediction or the very popular mid-week novena to Our Lady of Perpetual Succour. At school we were told that Mass and communion on nine consecutive first Fridays would insure heavenly acceptance when we died, but neither of my parents appeared to be much impressed by such a promise. Until I entered the convent I had never been to a Christmas Midnight Mass or participated in Holy Week liturgy, not even Good Friday Stations of the Cross.

At school I learnt about the things that set Catholics apart, beginning with braving the state school kids chanting 'Catholic dogs stink like frogs' as I passed them going to school in the other direction. By the time I was nine I could list the parts of the Mass but was totally ignorant of their deeper meaning or relevance to my life.

Cradle Catholic

Primary school religious education culminated in confirmation, which was presented as an opportunity to pick up my call to be a soldier of Christ. All up, with the exception of the gospel stories which I loved, and some Australian church history which may or may not have been historically correct, primary school religion classes were a mish-mash of religious information and catechism questions and answers. I could parrot the answers, understood little of what they meant and accepted all of it unquestioningly.

My all-girl secondary school religion was more of the same, accompanied by warnings about the danger of communism and a solemn mix of something known as apologetics which would enable me to defend the teachings of the Catholic faith in the eventuality of their being questioned. I left school knowing more about the history of devotion to the Sacred Heart than I did about the causes of World War I.

While school and the Catholic community gave me a grounding in the morals and rituals of Catholicism, home was where I absorbed Gospel values as they were lived out in the ordinary of day by day. My mother was gentle and patient, with her husband as well as with her children. She was a stay-at-home mum until she discovered the joys of golf and the company of other women, and a little timid, always standing in Dad's shadow. He was opinionated, interesting as well as being interested in the lives of others, ready to take on new challenges as long as they didn't involve eating vegetables. In his forties he went to Europe for the first time and only stopped travelling in his early nineties.

He had an Irish dislike for unearned authority and frequently voiced his opinions about political injustice in well-written letters to the daily papers. He read history and was a regular at adult education classes, loved a bargain, and in later years told all and sundry what

A Gentle Unfolding

spendthrifts his four children were. When I was clearing out his wardrobe after he died, I held his favourite shoes in my hands for a long time. Those shoes had travelled the world and walked him to daily Mass where he always sat well away from others so he didn't have to share the sign of peace. That was how my dad was! I knew that while I could never walk in my father's shoes, either literally or figuratively, my life journey and my faith journey are linked to his, and for that I give thanks.

I'm glad I was named Judith. Once you get the gory details of the biblical story out of the way, she comes across as brave, prayerful and a trifle sassy, someone I could appreciate as a role model. It has been suggested that she never existed, that her story is more of a parable or even a long-ago novel. But I am proud to carry the name of a scriptural woman. If I am to be faithful to the baptismal commitment my godmother and my parents made in my name then, like Judith, I need the courage to follow the dream that God planted in my soul, the space to nurture the relationship that goes hand in hand with God-dreams and a bit of her sass to challenge those in the church who would dismiss me as irrelevant and second class because I am a woman.

3
Little black dress

When God sends us seductive messages wrapped in feelings of deep peace like clear, quiet sunlight, we don't always know how to respond, or even if we need to. We dip into the wordless yearnings swirling around inside us and look for somewhere to put them. That's what my teenage self did.

In the religious either/or of the mid-twentieth century, feelings like that equalled a vocation to religious life. Religion's love affair was with words and correct ideas, not bringing people to recognise and appreciate the God-imprint we call spirituality. I looked to religion for a sign, a light, a path to God, and it offered me the off-the-shelf response – enter the convent.

My love affair with God was boosted by my first glimpse of the convent that would be my home for the next eighteen months. I had expected a large, sombre brick building, maybe set in sweeping lawns, but definitely ringed by a high brick fence. Instead I was delighted by a copycat English country house, with sloping roofs and attics and the Australian touch of a wraparound veranda. Instead of a keep-out kind of wall it was set in paddocks, with country style wire fences and the glint of a creek in the distance. My romantic soul was charmed, a feeling that would soon be tested by cramped, unheated rooms and

A Gentle Unfolding

chilblains during the bitterly cold winters of the New South Wales Southern Highlands.

For the next six months, while my left-behind peers were trying out boyfriends and deep in fashion speak, I was being inducted into the mechanics and language of religious life. I had left behind my given names, Judith Patricia, and my family name, Scully. I was now Sister Mary Andrina, a postulant, one of a group of fourteen young women between the ages of sixteen and twenty-nine, all of whom had a deep conviction that God was calling them to religious life.

Years before a little black dress was a must-have in female wardrobes it became my everyday garb. My brown hair was covered by a short veil usually slipping one way or another. The clothes I arrived in were whisked away to be stored in the large barn that was out of bounds to postulants and novices. Maybe they are still there, along with other discarded 1950s garments, a whole cache of vintage fashion.

The days passed in a blur of newness. Even though everything was so different and decidedly counter-cultural, I wasn't homesick for very long. The hard stuff – getting up early, the loss of family relationships and school friends, the grandma underwear – was offset by the fact that I was young, idealistic and unworldly, or maybe just naive. Whatever, I was quite sure that God needed me and that God and I were in for a wonderful future.

I was introduced to a smorgasbord of prayerful religious practices, most of them unfamiliar. Every day we prayed a modified version of the Prayer of the Church, known as the Office. There was morning meditation, particular examen at midday, as well as spiritual reading and private prayer, called adoration, and the rosary recited in common. All this praying was balanced by one hour after lunch and another after the evening meal, known as recreation, when talking was allowed. Feast days were marked by walks down to the Winge-

Little black dress

carribee River or a picnic. We put together concerts when the musical among us rewrote the words of the popular songs we had left behind, giving them a religious twist.

Learning to keep silent wasn't easy for a bunch of normal young women. It had been explained to us that keeping silence would help us focus our minds on God. Idle chatter of a gossipy nature was out, even during the permitted times of talking. Except on special occasions, meals were passed in silence, broken only by the voice of a novice reading aloud from some spiritual book or other.

As well as keeping our tongues quiet, we were expected to observe something that was called custody of the eyes. So we spent our days with downcast eyes, studiously avoiding looking at one another or noticing anything much around us. Living in harmony with others was not so difficult when close friendships were out and you weren't supposed to talk outside the recreation hour.

The original fourteen gradually became eleven. There would be an empty bed, a sign that someone had gone home, an absence not to be spoken about. Years later, when that empty bed was mine, that same silence still held. Community and love for one another was the ideal, but we were strongly discouraged from forming any deep friendships that might have replaced those we had left behind. Religious life kept some of its severest frowns for 'particular friendships'. Maybe the shame was that I kept that rule so well!

Summer came. I turned seventeen and my six months as a postulant was over. On 6 January, the feast of the Epiphany, my parents and younger brothers made the long car trip for a special ceremony, during which the local bishop formally presented me with a whole raft of black and white garments, known as the habit. Some of them starched, all of them bulky and uncomfortable and definitely not fashionable. I was now a novice. And I was happy.

A Gentle Unfolding

Nineteen-fifty-five was my novitiate year. McDonalds came to Australia and seat belts were made compulsory in all new cars. Scrabble came to Australia and after a major split in the Australian Labor Party the Democratic Labour Party came into being. And all of this passed right over my head.

The novice mistress, known as Mother Columcille, was as motherly as her title and a role model I would never outgrow. Years before it became common she brought a psychological dimension to the work of formation. She identified a passion in me that one day I would discover for myself. I cherish the letters she wrote to me over many years.

It was Mother Columcille who gave us regular classes where she spelt out the constitutions and explained the rules that underpinned the particular way the Daughters of Our Lady of the Sacred Heart were expected to live out God's call. The wording was formal but the spirit underlying the words was meant to bring us to a deeper appreciation of the love that God has for us and the ways in which we would endeavour to spread that love across the world.

We learnt about the history of the congregation, and its charism – the unique spirit and flavour that had flowed out of the founder's understanding of Gospel commitment. In 1854 a French priest, Jules Chevalier, had gathered a small group of men who, like himself, lived with an awareness that the whole of creation is a gift of God's love and that everything and everybody is sustained and cared for by God's compassionate love. He called his religious group Missionaries of the Sacred Heart, MSC for short. Twenty years later, with the help of a French widow, Marie-Louise Hartzer, he founded a sister congregation, to be named Daughters of Our Lady of the Sacred Heart.

In 1884, motivated by the motto that characterised the spirit of their congregation, *May the Sacred Heart of Jesus be everywhere loved*, five of these sisters, four French and one Irish, landed in Sydney, their

Little black dress

stepping stone to Papua New Guinea. Archbishop Moran offered them accommodation if they would agree to open a school for the children of Botany. I don't know whether any of that original five ever got as far as Papua New Guinea, but in the years that followed their Australian successors spread across Australia and other parts of the world.

I had become familiar with this spirituality while I was at school. It was heart spirituality and there was nothing harsh about it. Maybe that's why, most of the time, I loved my eighteen months of novitiate at Hartzer Park. I'm a romantic and a spirituality that focused on love helped me make light of a lot of traditional religious practices that in hindsight were ridiculous and not in the spirit of love. They had trickled down through the centuries, driven by images of a God who demanded a personal asceticism that would never be enough.

During my novitiate year, my mind absorbed a great deal of information about the vows of poverty, chastity and obedience, what was entailed, how they were to be lived out day by day, the solemnity and legality of it all. I understood the technicalities but the personal implications were beyond my experience. I'd had neither the joy nor the responsibility of handling my own finances. I'd never had a boyfriend or read a Mills & Boon romance and my sexual knowledge was sketchy at best. At this stage of my life I had a childlike perception of authority and would never have questioned it.

Intellectually I knew what I was doing, but it would be many years before I discovered that life-changing decisions need the powers of body, heart, imagination and past experience, not just the mind. Discernment is marked by doubt, hesitancy and middle of the night questions. I experienced none of that. I can only assume my religious superiors didn't either. If religious vows can be compared to marriage vows, then mine were probably illicit, made as they were without my fully informed consent.

A Gentle Unfolding

At the same time, those eighteen months defined and shaped the spirituality on which the rest of my life would be built. The convent discipline of times and places of silence would, over the years, lead me into deep places where God waits in the silence. Gently and persistently the formation I was given would change my image of God as distant, stern, all-seeing and white-bearded, to that of a loving, approachable if somewhat romanticised father figure. I would grow in appreciation of ritual as I saw it celebrated in the formulaic liturgy of Holy Week and through the imagery of Pentecost and Advent.

In our family photo album there is a shot of my mother and me taken the day of those first vows. There I am, all flowing black and white, my eighteen-year-old face encircled by a stiff coif, and there's my mum in a smart, tight-fitting suit, spike heels and red nails. That picture captures something of what I now understand about vocation.

Vocation is a trust in something way bigger than the imagination can capture. In its first heady romantic moments it has no real understanding or idea of the cost. My mother's spike heels and red nails didn't stand a chance against God, who accepted my vows of poverty, chastity and obedience and was prepared to let me grow into them. Vocation is not about the what, but the Who.

4

A suitcase of whites

For many, Sydney evokes tourist bureau images of a harbour presided over by a coathanger-shaped bridge, criss-crossing ferries and a white-sailed opera house. Sydney in the mid-1950s was a whole new world to me, and the only bit of it I saw was from the top floor of a Kensington convent. Where the opera house would one day show off its beauty, there was still a deep hole. I remember steamy summers, the enormous dormitory tucked under the attic roof where the young sisters slept, two years of teacher training, and the endless cooing of the pigeons that roosted on the upstairs verandas.

A two-hour train trip separated the novitiate from this large brick convent, built on a hill in suburban Sydney. Here five of us who had been together in the novitiate would spend two years learning how to face a class, be the teacher instead of the pupil. Our teacher training was in-house and the room set aside for it quickly became an oasis in the impersonal life of what was a large busy convent.

I started to make little discoveries about myself and to speak with my own voice, to the extent that the somewhat autocratic religious education lecturer failed my final paper because I wrote too much of it

A Gentle Unfolding

in my own words instead of hers. The sinking feeling this gave me was quickly overtaken by a spurt of personal satisfaction.

Despite this mini revolt, I passed the rest of the required examinations and taught a final lesson to the inspector's satisfaction. In due course a Victorian certificate arrived qualifying me to teach in every state of Australia. I was appointed to teach in Melbourne at a very new school, St Agnes's in East Moorabbin. This meant I would be living at Bentleigh where I had gone to school. It was strange to see the swarms of brown and gold-clad girls coming and going and to be living in what used to be the out-of-bounds convent. It also meant that occasionally I was able to see my family.

Teaching is something I love but haven't always enjoyed, and my first class really pushed me – just under a hundred preps in one room. I did my best, but apart from some great action songs and lots of stories I can't imagine that they learnt very much. I could have done with an occasional helpful word, but the school principal, known to me from novitiate days when she was the assistant novice mistress, was never much good at encouragement.

As the three years of my first profession came to an end I felt unsettled. Final profession loomed, when I would vow poverty, chastity and obedience for ever. Living the vows I had made wasn't difficult, mostly because I hadn't yet twigged that there was an inner dimension to these three aspects of the religious life.

Poverty I found easy because it wasn't really a choice – my basic needs were being met and I couldn't see beyond that. I had no idea what it was like to live on a budget or pay a bill, and I sat down to three nutritious, if not always tasty, meals a day, none of which I had to prepare.

Chastity was equally uncomplicated. In the absence of radio, film and novels my imagination was able to focus on things religious and

A suitcase of whites

the only males I ever saw were elderly priests assigned to say Mass each day in our chapel.

Obedience was showing signs of becoming a bit of a drag – permission was needed to do something as ordinary as go to my bedside cabinet for a clean handkerchief during the day. Furthermore, I was beginning to understand that living in a community of women with a broad range of age and temperament had its ups and downs, occasionally leavened by the humour and ease of some of the older sisters who hadn't let years of religious life squash their personalities. Those women touched into something in me that I was vaguely beginning to recognise as *being myself* – without knowing exactly what that might mean.

As the school year was ending I turned twenty-one and was permitted to celebrate it at home with my family, before returning to Kensington to prepare to make my final vows. That initially meant a formal interview with the provincial, Mother Concepta. She was very tall and severe looking and I don't recall ever seeing her smile. I found her more than a bit scary. She asked me if I was looking forward to making vows that would be life-long.

I knew I was feeling unsettled. I put my unease down to the fact that my twelve months' teaching hadn't been easy. Both the school principal and the convent superior were prickly kind of women, not generous with kind words. Then again, it might have been the pressure of being back in my home town and close to my family. Whatever it was, for the first time I was questioning my vocation.

I took a deep breath and told her I wasn't sure that making final vows was what I wanted to do. She looked at me over the top of her glasses and said, 'Everybody feels like that before final vows. Don't take any notice of it. Next year we're sending you to the missions, to Darwin.'

A Gentle Unfolding

That was all. End of interview. No discernment on her part and no follow through on mine. On 6 January 1959, aged twenty-one, I vowed poverty, chastity and obedience for ever, had my photo taken, received my mission cross and said goodbye to my family.

In a spirit of obedience shot through with barely suppressed excitement, I flew across Australia on my first ever plane ride, landing twelve hours later in a blast of tropical heat at Darwin airport. I arrived with a suitcase of white habits and a head full of white woman know-how, ready to educate the Aboriginal children of the Northern Territory into a better future.

At the time I never thought to ask the Aboriginal community how might be the best way to do that. My idealism sagged a little when I arrived at Port Keats, my first appointment, and the sandflies from the appropriately named Sandfly Creek sent out messages that there was fresh southern blood up at the Mission. But I survived, eventually moving on to the football-famous Bathurst Island, followed by a semester in the Red Centre at Santa Teresa, and, lastly, a couple of years on the Daly River.

Mission living introduced me to a life way beyond my limited religious and suburban experience. Novitiate and teacher training had done little to prepare me for the workload and responsibilities that I had to assume. I was teaching in a school where English was a second language, educational supplies were inadequate and the reading books supplied inappropriate. Most of the children had chronic ear infections and I quickly learnt to identify spots that might indicate leprosy. But the biggest drawback to their education was me. I did not speak the local Aboriginal language, and I was so ignorant I didn't even consider it a drawback.

Events like the assassination of John Kennedy, the building of the Berlin wall and the Beatles' visit to Australia barely touched me in the

A suitcase of whites

remote Northern Territory. Vatican II came and went, leaving behind possibilities and new directions as well as unrest in its wake, and feminists were beginning to make their voices heard. I rejoiced when the restrictive heart-shaped headgear I'd worn since 1955 was replaced with a simple white veil and the habit lost some of its weighty folds.

Day by day I continued to inculcate European values and lifestyle into the lives of Aboriginal girls, young women who would marry in their mid to late teens and be expected to live in huts without furniture or running water. I taught them to pray in English to a God that they probably assumed had white skin. I never asked them about their own deep Aboriginal spirituality. I didn't even know it was there.

As a small OLSH community, we did our best to stick to the regular prayer times and practices that were seen as essential to every good religious sister. However a regular convent timetable was not possible when there were babies to deliver, bread to be baked and a communal dining room to supervise three times a day. Sandflies and mosquitoes disturbed my morning meditation and a baking hot church in the afternoon made private prayer a chore. Even the annual retreat in Darwin was boring and somehow irrelevant in the heat and silence that surrounded it. My prayer life was a kind of lifeless routine amid the challenge and deep satisfaction of living on a remote mission station. And I had no idea that my prayer and my ministry needed to be a whole.

Towards the end of the 1960s, a young priest newly appointed to the Northern Territory casually suggested that the language and culture of the Aboriginal people we were serving should be a starting point for evangelisation, not the reverse. He could see no reason why the art, the dance, the music of the Aboriginal people shouldn't have a place in the regular mission liturgies. He began learning the local dialect. Maybe because we were both young, he thought I would share

A Gentle Unfolding

his perceptions. But I was indignant. Beneath my polite exterior I simmered with resentment. A newcomer, inexperienced, coming in and wanting to change things!

The buzzword in Aboriginal Affairs during the 1960s was assimilation. We, the educated ones, the ones with the know-how, knew what was best for Australia's first people. I'd never questioned it. Now a priest I respected, who shared the same religious background as me, was implying that the Aboriginal people had something that latecomers to Australia didn't — a story, a spirituality and a culture that went back into time. More, all that was worthy of respect. For someone like me, accustomed to a them-and-us approach, this was unsettling.

Nothing happened straight away and a seed planted by the words of that brash young priest grew so slowly and out of sight that I didn't know it was there. It wasn't his words as such, prophetic though they might have been, but his respect for the dignity of the Aboriginal people that shone through them and touched something in me that I would only recognise gradually

5

Mission memories

As a child, I put my pennies and threepences into a money box to 'buy a black baby for God', terminology that was typical of the times. That, coupled with reading the children's page in *The Far East*, a monthly magazine full of missionary doings, was the extent of my missionary interest. That was, until my novice year when I got a bit of a crush on a French missionary known as Bishop Henry Verius. He was a fine looking man with a black bushy beard who'd died young, worn out by only nine years of missionary work, dysentery and malaria on a speck of land off the Papua New Guinea coastline known as Yule Island. In the full flush of religious and missionary fervour, helped along by teenage romanticism, I decided that I was destined for the missions, Yule Island in particular. There I would follow in Henry's self-sacrificing footsteps.

Of course that's not what happened. Instead of Yule Island I was sent to Port Keats, now known as Wadeye, an Aboriginal settlement 230 kilometres south-west of Darwin, and then only accessible by air or, during the dry season, by boat as long as you didn't mind getting seasick. I'd arrived still feeling a little cheated out of my idealistic dreams about Papua New Guinea, but it didn't take long to realise that the space, the endless horizon, the silence, the rusts and browns

A Gentle Unfolding

of the dry season and the vivid greens of the wet and the miles of unmarked coastal sand that edged a blue, blue sea, had stimulated my inner DNA.

Even though I would go on to teach in four different Aboriginal mission settlements, the way each was staffed and run was similar. Staffing was a joint responsibility of MSC priests and brothers and the OLSH sisters, with one of the priests being appointed as superintendent. There were three, sometimes four, sisters living in community – a nurse who was matron of the mission hospital, a housekeeper who was responsible for the communal mission kitchen, and one or two teachers. The layout of each mission station was similar – the church, centered between the presbytery and the convent, kitchen and bakehouse, boys' and girls' dormitories, well apart, and the hospital a little beyond that, while the Aboriginal camp was a short walk away.

It was geographical them and us. The MSCs and we sisters might have had a common founder and religious charism, but the sharing stopped there. There were no feast day meals or socialising, and in twelve years I never saw the inside of the MSC house, known as the presbytery. I appreciated the presence and company of the men who lived in it. Living as we did in such close proximity, I had plenty of opportunity to recognise their masculine foibles and be alternatively amused and annoyed by them. Mostly though I appreciated just knowing they were there, sharing the same focus, the same vocation. My days were too busy and too disciplined for anything else.

When staffing was increased to include other women and men, voluntary workers known as lay missionaries, I'm ashamed to say that except for an occasional polite greeting we sisters all but ignored them. Now and again I would see pretty underwear and cool sleeve-

Mission memories

less tops and dresses on the clothesline outside the house where the female voluntary workers were housed, and I would experience a stab of envy. They were doing God's work in shorts and top, why not me?

As religious women, we were set apart. A renowned anthropologist, Dr William Stanner, who was making a study of the Murinbata people, the original inhabitants of the Port Keats area, sometimes shared his findings and deep appreciation of Aboriginal culture with the male staff, but not with us. That was our fault, and eventually our loss.

Similarly, I never visited the Aboriginal camp. There was an expectation that the people who lived in the camp would come to us, not the other way around. Some nights I would be lulled to sleep by the distant sounds of the didgeridoo and clapping sticks, but I never attended a corroboree.

The ink on my teacher's registration had barely dried when I took charge of the girls' school at Port Keats. Built on stilts, it was a rough timber building with push-out timber shutters and furnished with long narrow tables and stools. Once they reached school age, the children moved into dormitory accommodation, girls close to the convent, boys under the not quite so watchful eye of the male staff. Educating boys and girls separately seemed to have been a Catholic thing, or maybe it was tribal. Whatever it was, I didn't teach Aboriginal boys until I went to Daly River ten years later. Education-wise the years became a blur. I was just one person with an Aboriginal assistant trying to teach basic reading, writing and numeracy – sometimes creatively, mostly desperately – to girls for whom English was a second language.

Such day-to-day difficulties were superseded by a host of memorable times and experiences. In the Wet there was water – everywhere. The children would pile into an old war-time Blitz truck or scramble onto a trailer behind a tractor and find someone to drive it deep into

A Gentle Unfolding

the bush. Once there they would have a wonderful afternoon diving in and out of a deep waterhole fed by a waterfall. During the Dry season there were beaches that stretched for miles where the girls would fish or dig in the mangroves for crab, then barbecue them. Seafood would never taste that good again.

Twice a week the most technically advanced member of staff, usually one of the brothers, would rev up the generator and spool up one of an aging stock of films. Sometimes the projector didn't even break down! The children and adults sat on the ground, the sisters got fold-up chairs and together we clapped, cheered, oohed and aahed our way through the film. Even today I can recognise a John Wayne movie within seconds. Then it was on to dormitory duty, making sure the girls were secure for the night and the boys safely back in their own area.

There were annual events – presents and new clothes at Christmas, sports days in Darwin, the annual eisteddfod, more often than not topped by a mission choir. Those kids could sing! One year, in the absence of a more experienced musician, it was me with my back to the audience and the choir before me. Predictably, we didn't get a place but it didn't seem to matter. Darwin was an exciting place for children who rarely saw shops or paved streets and only wore shoes once a year. Once Slim Dusty came to Daly River for a concert and the whole place buzzed with excitement.

If I loved the wide open space of Port Keats, I equally enjoyed living on an island – Bathurst Island, one of the Tiwi islands. The Tiwi islanders were exuberant and noisy. Even their looks differed from mainland Aboriginals. The 2009 film, *Australia*, had a brief scene that showed the original mission church on Bathurst Island. I was taken by surprise and for a moment I was back there in the darkness of the shutter-clad building. My prayer time in that church had often been

Mission memories

distracted by the desire to consign those dark, heavy, hand-hewn timber shutters to the mission kitchen fire and replace them with Territory-style glass louvres.

I remembered the narrow strait between the islands where crocodiles lurked and prevented adventurous children from swimming between the two. I heard kids screaming as a sneaky snake crawled up the back of my folding chair while I was enjoying a musical from the 1940s. I'll never forget trying to teach close on a hundred small child-ren who had limited English and even less experience of discipline. We did a lot of singing! And on a deeper level I still appreciate a birthday when one of the sisters in my little community packed me a lunch and sent me out into the bush for a blissful day by myself.

My family visited, first my dad on his way back from visiting Europe, later on my mother and lastly my youngest brother Mike. The children mobbed each one, sung for them, hung on to their hands and shyly stroked my mother's soft skin, marvelled that Mike and I had 'same mother, same father'. Only once during my years in the Northern Territory did I return south for a holiday.

I had landed in Darwin young, enthusiastic, full of religious fervour and the unchallenged arrogance of ignorance, protected as it was by the habit and veil I wore. Twelve years on, I found myself envying the Aboriginal women because they seemed to be so comfortable in their own skin. I was discovering that the Aboriginal women I had met and worked with over the years had what I can only describe as womanly dignity.

Dignity is an inner thing. It can't be quantified and you can't learn it from a book. It's something passed down through the generations, to be owned and lived. Seen in passing, these women were unsophisticated, poorly dressed and often uneducated, without the trappings of makeup and jewellery. But I'd watch them laughing, talking with

A Gentle Unfolding

each other, nonchalantly caring for their children, and I envied their womanliness. Beside them I felt like an inexperienced girl.

I became aware of yearnings that I couldn't or wouldn't name. Without knowing there was a word for it I began to learn discernment, looking beneath the surface of what was and wondering what lay there, what was God's voice and what was mine – did the two sometimes become one?

For years my prayer life had been according to the book, correct but lifeless. I was living behind the veneer of my life and I wanted to have a chance to be the whole person. My religious congregation was little help. Since Vatican II there had been many changes in religious life but the OLSH Sisters had been slow to embrace them. That young priest who a few years back had challenged the way we did things had sowed a seed in me and now it had split and was showing signs of life.

When the major superior next made one of her official visits, known as visitation, she told me that I was to be sent south for … Well, I never did hear what my congregation had in store for me. I asked instead for twelve months leave, known as exclaustration. Sensibly, she asked why. The only response I was able to give was – 'I feel like I'm a square peg in a round hole.' Neither then, nor later on, did any OLSH sister attempt to talk with me about my decision, which in hindsight I find insulting.

When the requisite formalities were completed I returned to Melbourne, leaving behind my habit and veil neatly folded on my bed. The suitcase I'd arrived with was almost empty, but within me were the gifts of those years, unexpected, tightly-wrapped, gifts that would be years in the unwrapping.

6

'Here be dragons …'

Long ago, mapmakers used to write these words at the place where their map stopped. Fear of the unknown hides behind images and dragons were imaged as composites of the unknown and unexperienced. It didn't matter that nobody had ever actually seen a dragon, for even the smallest child knew that they were to be feared. Safety lay in the familiar, the known.

The minute I walked off the plane from Darwin, I felt like I was in dragon territory. The faces surrounding me might have been family but they were unfamiliar, some of them brand new, some wearing the signs of age. The airport was noisy, my knee-length orange crimplene dress was scratchy as well as an unfamiliar length and I was aware that I needed a good haircut. Most difficult of all, when my dad said, 'Let's go home', home wasn't the home of my childhood but a different house in an unfamiliar suburb.

The world I walked into was full of ordinary things I'd never done. The first Australian supermarkets had opened in 1960 but I'd never shopped in one. I'd never eaten Asian food, been to a party, drunk beer or sipped a glass of wine. I'd never had a bank account, or been shopping for clothes and had no idea how to apply makeup. Since I'd left school I'd never had a close friend, made a casual phone call.

A Gentle Unfolding

People talked about Graham Kennedy and Mavis Bramston and I had no idea why this man and woman were seen as celebrities. I'd never watched TV. I'd never worn slacks, gone on holiday or talked casually to any man who didn't preface his name with Father or Brother.

I had been granted twelve months leave from my religious community. Called by that unfriendly name, exclaustration, it was time out, a chance to test drive what was a major decision, a space in which to pray and reflect on the enormity of my request to be released from religious vows. While still bound by those vows of poverty, chastity and obedience, I was expected to support myself financially. What I did day to day with my time would be up to me and no longer decided by a convent timetable or religious superior. And, until I was released from my vow of chastity, dating was not really an option.

In my experience of religious life, exclaustration was shrouded in silence, spoken about in whispers. Living as I did on a remote mission station I'd never been party to any quiet gossip that floated through suburban convents when a bed was suddenly left empty. I didn't know anyone who had taken advantage of it. But I soon found out what it was like.

During that year, while I searched for what I believed was a more authentic life and adjusted to being called Judith or Miss Scully instead of Sister, there was no communication between myself and the OLSH Sisters. No letters or phone calls from anyone in the religious congregation that had been my life, almost my family, since I was sixteen. It was appropriate that my last night in the Northern Territory had been spent at the convent in the grounds of the Darwin leprosarium. The shunning I experienced during my year of exclaustration reminded me of women and men, some familiar to me, who had been diagnosed with leprosy and banished from their community to spend years in the leprosarium. In another way I too had become one of 'the disappeared'.

'Here be dragons ...'

On that early morning flight out of Darwin I left behind my young adult years and the unmarked skin of that youth. However I took with me a very useful Victorian teaching certificate and something not quite as useful – a working knowledge of liturgy, scripture, prayer and church-speak. I had survived living in a small community in a remote area of Australia without the benefits of hot water, electricity and salad vegetables. Seventeen years of convent living had gifted me with a disciplined approach to neat and tidy and a grudging appreciation of structure. I had arrived as a girl and left as a woman-in-the-making. If my years in religious life could be summed up as black and white, then the year that followed it was streaked with colour.

It was January and a new school year was about to begin. I needed to support myself financially so I took a deep breath and faced one of those dragons. It meant ringing the Melbourne Catholic Education department, braving the unfamiliar transport system and for the first time ever having to be interviewed before being offered a teaching position. I discovered that there was nothing to fear from this dragon and walked out of the building with a job offer in my bag. It was 1972 and employment was easy to come by.

For the first few months I lived with my parents and taught a Grade 4 class in a neighbouring Catholic school. After twelve years teaching Aboriginal children it took me a few days to adjust to a class full of fair-skinned children, all of whom spoke English. Gradually I settled down and began to enjoy the new experience of having no responsibility for my pupils once the school day was over. Spare time was an unaccustomed luxury.

Staff relationships were a bit more problematic. I didn't know how to relate to the worldly and confident young women who made up the school staff. They seemed so flippant to my structured way

A Gentle Unfolding

of viewing daily life. I had no small talk, no shared memories, and certainly no practice in the throwaway remarks that floated around the staff room.

This wasn't surprising. When lay missionaries had begun working in Catholic missions in the mid-1960s, we sisters were advised to be polite but impersonal. It was another them-and-us approach and while I would have liked the friendship of those wonderful young women and men my religious training had impressed on me that we who had answered God's call to religious life were special, set apart. Relationships with lay people, especially young males, was a no-no.

That year was full of firsts. I sorted out who was who among sisters-in-law, nephews and nieces and other assorted family. I learnt to manage my finances, saving enough money to buy a second-hand car, a red Mini, and celebrated this milestone with a Christmas Eve driving licence. I explored, or maybe exploited, the joys of shopping and experimented with clothes that accentuated that I was a woman. I was invited to a ball, my first, and I bought a long yellow tulle dress for it, a garment that years later would end up in my daughters' dress-up box.

The freedom I was experiencing was intoxicating. There was so much life to catch up with, people to meet, suburbs to explore, books to read, TV to watch. I let myself be carried along, shedding religious practices as though they had never been part of my life. Long-suppressed feelings bubbled up inside me. I rented a flat in the inner suburb of Collinwood and something about the silence and aloneness that accompanied living by myself shifted beyond the imposed silence of religious life practices and into a solitude that wasn't lonely but life-giving.

As I moved away from what had been my geographic and physical centre for so many years I began hearing God's voice in a different way

'Here be dragons ...'

— not the way of religious obedience, tied up in traditions and practices that blurred the bigger picture, but centred on life as it was unfolding around me. I experienced a wordless 'but wait, there's more' feeling, like standing outside a locked door without the key. I was just beginning to understand that the key was Vatican II.

When Pope John XXIII opened the first session of Vatican II in September of 1963 I was totally absorbed in the day-to-day happenings of a remote mission station in outback Australia, a whole world away from the deliberations of two thousand bishops. Changes crept into the way liturgy was celebrated and religious orders like mine began updating their constitutions and rules.

Some time during the late 1960s, I was given a large paperback containing all sixteen documents of Vatican II. I made a half-hearted attempt to read them, but the unfamiliar language and the length of the sentences tired me. I ignored the connections that lay between the words I was reading, the challenges and difficulties that were part and parcel of mission life and my own increasing unsettledness. In the words of poet Marge Piercy, I was 'drinking wine from a sieve'.

The connections must have gone underground, like the roots of a deep planted seed, because during this gap year of exclaustration Vatican II started to come alive for me. I don't know how it happened. Maybe it was stimulated by inservice days that introduced me to new ways of teaching religious education. Possibly it was homilies that I found stimulating. I was suddenly alive to the fact that the church was a people of God, that evangelisation was not the exclusive province of priests and nuns and brothers, that it was a collaborative affair. It excited me.

Naturally enough there were days when this wonderful newness didn't satisfy me and then I'd retreat into feeling that I had let God down, that leaving had been a mistake, that I'd lost my vocation, it

A Gentle Unfolding

was all my fault. But as my exclaustration year neared its end I knew that I had no desire to return to religious life.

Those years hadn't been a mistake, nor were they wasted. I hadn't lost my vocation, because God's call was still strong in me. I just had to trust where it might lead. Gradually new possibilities would unfold out of what had seemed like failure.

7
Cloud walking

In my convent days, the only clothing dilemma I ever had was the choice between clean or maybe it'll do another day. Now, more often than not, I stand in front of an open wardrobe and sigh because everything in it is either too tight, out of date, too hot or cool – just not right. It describes how I increasingly felt as my year teaching Grade 4 was drawing to an end. Just as a favourite dress has to be laid aside when a more mature shape means it no longer fits, the way I had lived out my response to God's call was no longer the right fit.

The years immediately following Vatican II had been a time of enormous growth in the Australian church. The council documents had opened the floodgates to an understanding of the moral freedom and responsibility that came with sacramental baptism, not just ordination or religious profession. God's call to lay ministry and discipleship echoed in a multitude of willing listeners and the possibilities seemed excitingly satisfying. Large numbers of women and men left the priesthood and religious life and picked up their God call in ways that better suited their individuality. The stigma formerly attached to such a move gradually vanished, making the change culturally accept-

A Gentle Unfolding

able, though I still come across people who attach expectations to me 'because you were a nun'.

I had begun to hear God's voice in a different way – not the way of religious obedience, tied down by traditions and practices that blurred the bigger picture, but one that was broader and deeper. By moving beyond the limits within which I had lived since novitiate days I had stirred a sleeping dragon inside me into fire. Discovering the dignity inherent in the Aboriginal women I saw on the mission settlements had put me in touch with the creative freedom that lay hidden beneath the layers of my religious observance. The passion for God that led me to the novitiate had gradually been usurped, tamped down and devalued and I yearned to get it back. Like the mythical dragon, I was all fired up.

It was a Pentecost feeling, a mixture of relief and euphoria, relief that I had made the decision to leave and an excitement about whatever was waiting to be brought into being. I was intensely conscious of the fire within me. It enlivened me, sometimes took my breath away, connected me with the web of life that I hadn't ever really touched before. I saw endless possibilities in people and story and music and I longed to bring it all together.

The spirituality that infused religious life had cautioned me to transcend feelings and emotions like this, to lay them aside, 'give them to God', or 'offer them up'. For years I had struggled with the bubbles of enthusiasm and get-up-and-go that I experienced. I'd never learnt to listen to myself and to trust what I found there. Until my last year in the Northern Territory, I'd assumed my 'Is this all there is?' feelings were inappropriate, something to be overcome, to be ignored or suffered in silence until I could return to a static kind of inner peace.

For ordinary women like me, religious life before Vatican II was very cautious. It was safe; risk-taking and decisions were left to reli-

Cloud walking

gious superiors. The God-fire that powered women like the founder of the Sisters of St Joseph, Mary MacKillop, or Marie-Louise Hartzer, the founder of the Daughters of Our Lady of the Sacred Heart, had become bogged in the everydayness of ministry and canonical requirements.

Caution inhibits impulsive responses and eventually all but kills the passion that fires them, and I came from a family where caution was valued. My father didn't call it that but described it as the remedy for impulsive behaviour, while I saw my responses as intuitive. He saw intuition as a kind of magic phenomenon, but hunches are formed out of our past experiences and knowledge. So while relying on gut feelings may not always lead to good decisions, it's not nearly as flighty a tactic as it may sound. I saw my intuition as difficult to verbalise, a mixture of head, heart and body that I hoped was something to do with God. Nevertheless, to his dying day my father told me that I was too impulsive, in circumstances ranging from supermarket shopping to buying a house. Strangely, he never once advised caution around my decision to seek a dispensation from my religious vows.

Caution may be a trait that the Scully family and religious congregations found comfortable, but once I left the security of religious life behind it began to lose its hold on me. Moving away from what had been my centre had freed me to hear God's voice in new and different ways. My feet had left the ground and I was walking on clouds, free to voice opinions, to be self-reliant, to make choices about how and where I lived, to pick and choose religious practices, to let my creativity out.

Most cloud walkers are closet mystics, not a label many feel good enough to claim. Writer Kathleen Norris says that when someone is described as being a mystic it's generally meant as a warning – here is somebody whose head is in the clouds and can't get to places on time, someone we admire but wouldn't want our children to marry.

A Gentle Unfolding

Cloud walking is just the kind of expression that drives pragmatists mad. I have a hunch that there are a lot of undiagnosed mystics around, women and men who are embarrassed by the God-pull they feel. Fearing the scorn – or, worse, indifference – of others to something so counter-cultural and personal, they tuck God into an appropriately labelled box, to be taken out on formal occasions. The remainder of the time that pull stays deep within them, private and a little shameful because emotive responses to God are not the done thing. And all the time they feel God nudging, pushing, inviting them to let go and cloud walk.

If you want to cloud walk then you have to be gutsy enough to step out into what feels like the unknown but actually is moving into the innerness of what is already known. So, as my exclaustration year drew to a close, I knew it was time for me to move on. I wrote the necessary letters and in time received formal documentation from the Sacred Congregation for Religious and Secular Institutes releasing me from my vows of poverty, chastity and obedience.

Religious life gifted me with things that have endured through the years. I value prayer as an expression of relationship with God and the God image in me, but not the pious words and practices that seemingly enclosed it. These I shed as easily as my left-behind religious habit. I will never forget the women who shared my life, for their small kindnesses and the example of Gospel values lived day by day, sometimes in difficult circumstances. I admire them for the risks they took in staying within their religious vows for years and the time they spent in places that tested their faith as well as their health. And, if I'm an economical housekeeper it's because I learnt it in the convent.

I could have continued primary school teaching, but I needed more. I began scanning the classifieds in the Catholic papers, look-

Cloud walking

ing for something that would jump out at me, set my heart racing, a jigsaw piece that would fit into the God-space that religious life hadn't quite filled. And then I found it.

The Good Samaritan Sisters had advertised for someone to join them in a venture called the Motor Mission, which involved taking religious education classes and sacramental preparation into government schools and after-school classes across eight parishes. As I read the newspaper ad I felt a tingle of excitement. Maybe the mention of mission had something to do with that. I applied, was interviewed and offered the position. I said goodbye to my Grade 4 class, thanked my parents for their hospitality, packed my little red car with my year of dedicated shopping and moved into a one-bedroomed flat. As January came to an end I began a new job.

On first glance, working full time in religious education with two sisters looked like more of the same, especially as my some of my exit experience had left me feeling bruised and somewhat ashamed that I had let down the women I had accepted and loved as my religious family.

The two sisters who interviewed me were open and friendly, not only accepting of my background but valuing what I could bring to this new venture. Their excitement as they talked about pioneering a new way of bringing religious education to the growing number of Catholic children who were being educated in government schools was infectious. I caught its possibilities, and in saying goodbye to regular classroom teaching I made a decision that would ripple its way through my life.

8

Motor Mission

The Motor Mission was appropriately named. Four catechists, two of them Good Samaritan sisters and the other two lay women, zipped from parish to parish by car providing religious education for Catholic children who attended government schools. Centred in the Melbourne suburb of Reservoir, it was a creative and challenging post Vatican II response to a pressing need for faith education in the rapidly growing Melbourne suburbs.

Our salaries were met by the parishes in which we worked, and we both supported and were supported in turn by volunteer catechists. I worked alongside Sister Marguerite, a larger-than-life character, an enthusiast who overwhelmed and engaged me with the exuberance and passion that accompanied everything she did.

Every morning and part of the afternoon was taken up with religion lessons in four different neighbourhood government schools. Each student was entitled to thirty minutes a week of religious education. Catholics went to one room, non-Catholics to another and the children who were neither were not sure where they were supposed to be.

We taught from weekly hand-out sheets, a program called *Let's Go Together*. They were excellent – colourful, relevant, scriptural and

Motor mission

practical, and Australian. But between comings and goings and roll calls, the half hour was more like twenty minutes, which was frustrating because lessons ended up being a race to get through the wealth of possibilities that the sheets presented. Preparation for reconciliation, first communion and confirmation was held in after-school classes, usually in a parish hall or one of the Catholic school classrooms.

It would be nice to say that teaching a religious education class in a government school was rewarding and appreciated by the children, and sometimes it was. The younger children listened wide-eyed to Jesus stories and prayed earnestly for their families, but the older students were not always quite so receptive. Officially these classes were about the Catholic religion, not a space where children were given the opportunity to touch into their personal experience of God. The half an hour time slot was not long enough for me to become familiar with the children's names, let alone allow space for the topic to be integrated into their own story And having the class teacher hovering about inhibited me.

After-school sacramental classes were an opportuniuty to introduce children to the Jesus of the gospels, to share the riches of the Catholic tradition, to experience communal prayer. But it's difficult to be enthusiastic about the wonders of sacramental theology when you're just a kid, the school day is over and you're tired and hungry.

As the newness of my employment wore off, I realised that I was uncomfortable with the idea of faith education being a subject to be taught in a school classroom along with English and maths. It seemed to be missing the point, though I struggled to find words to spell out just what that point was. Motor mission was throwing up more questions than answers, none of which I could effectively answer.

What it was doing was laying the groundwork for my future ministry. Despite the customary practice of out-sourcing the religious

A Gentle Unfolding

education of children, I believed that it was not only a parental right to educate their child in faith but their responsibility. Confining that education to a primary school classroom was separating the child's baptismal relationship with God from the ordinary events of family and community life. For the first time I had niggling doubts about the church's focus on education of the young. Growth in faith is life-long. It doesn't stop at Grade 6 or even Year 12.

As I saw it, it was the task of the church to assist parents to educate their children in faith, not the reverse. I was disappointed that the finance and creativity that went into Catholic schools was not also given to adult and parent faith education. But mostly I kept such counter-cultural thoughts to myself, while first communions and confirmations came and went, and so did the children.

I needed some religious education of my own as whatever theology I understood was more intuitive than bookish or academic. During my year teaching Grade 4 I had attended a semester of lectures which made scripture come alive in ways that seventeen years of morning meditation had rarely done. In the novitiate I had been taught how to meditate on a gospel passage. In the years that followed, I faithfully followed the process the novice mistress gave us: first, slowly read a passage from the gospel and try to get a sense of its characters and geography. Second, ask yourself what message does this passage have for you? And, last, talk to God about what you experienced.

It was a good method but it was a bit like a comprehension exercise and no one ever said to me, 'Wait, there's more.' It was only when I attended that semester of lectures about teaching scripture that I discovered there was an innerness to scripture that matched the need inside me.

As I tried to bring gospel stories to life for primary school-aged children, somehow the deeper meaning in scripture began to touch

Motor mission

into my whole self, not just my head. I began to enjoy the scriptural connections I was experiencing, and my imagination supplied colourful details and relevant experiences that found their way out of my life into religion classes and back again into my life in new and rewarding ways. I'd found a new outlet for the dragon fire within.

I became one of the women and men, mostly women, who were attending theology lectures designed to equip them to be catechists. Lectures were a cerebral process. The presenter was entertaining, but the matter he – most often he – had to impart was heavy with church-speak and I'd find myself engaged in planning my winter wardrobe or compiling a shopping list instead of attentively taking notes. Faithfully, week after week for a whole year, I turned up, eventually collecting a certificate giving me formal permission to do what I had been doing all along, teach RE. Despite my inattention, I now had a slightly better understanding of what it was I was trying to do.

The very best theology lecture I've ever had was given by a Grade 6 boy in one of my state school classes. It was the kind of class I dreaded. The students were disruptive and cheeky and it was a struggle to maintain order let alone teach them anything. I tried using one of those lines that trip off the tongue and sound religious. I said something to the effect that God is like a loving Father. This one boy heard me, stopped firing paper pellets or whatever it was he was doing and said, 'You've got to be joking, Miss. You dunno my old man.' I never did know that boy's name but I have never forgotten his words. A child's formative experience of God comes through the loving touch of parents. If that hasn't happened, pious words will never replace it. Church-speak has a lot to answer for.

Sister Marguerite, my work partner, loved stories, and I caught her enthusiastic love and respect for children's literature. She showed me how to use picture books to help children – and adults too –

A Gentle Unfolding

make sense of the complexity of life in all its stages and experiences, to recognise God in what can be flicked away as too ordinary to be of value.

The simple words of a children's storybook like Dyan Sheldon and Gary Blythe's *The Whale's Song,* one of my favourites, can highlight the call each one of us hears to live out the dream God plants deep within. Today I still trawl the children's shelves in bookshops, marvelling at the artwork, the simplicity of the wording and the depth of meaning implicit in so few pages.

For specific reasons that escape me now, I fell out with Sister Marguerite. It was probably to do with my growing unease that RE classes in government schools were not the best use of time, energy or finance, or my belief that an energetic post Vatican II church needed to come up with more user-friendly ways to spread the Good News of the Gospel. It didn't go down well.

I liked working with her but I was expected to know my place and that attitude was not about to change. This was a Good Samaritan ministry and I wasn't to question it. Possibly I wasn't even qualified to do so, but at the time I didn't have the self-knowledge to recognise that. After three eventful – and for me – fruitful years working on motor mission it was time to go.

Those three years had flown by. I'd fallen in love with someone who didn't return my affection, moved into a shared apartment with the doubtful address of 100 Easey Street, clashed with my partner in ministry and married the man with whom I would share my life for twenty-five years before he died with motor neurone disease.

Some things in my life had changed a great deal during those three years, but my head and my heart still had no idea how to talk to one another. I had been aware of God all around me, but not in touch with God within me. Working with three women, two of whom were

Motor mission

religious sisters in touch with the world around them, had grown me up a little. Now my more mature, emerging self was starting to engage with the messiness that underlies the ordinary. God was gently nudging me into the future when I would begin to look beneath the surface, to engage with the inwardness of everyday encounters and activities.

9

Mothering

When I first met Terry he was a shy, lanky fifteen-year-old, more interested in football than girls. Then I disappeared into religious life and he went to work in the insurance industry. Twenty years later we met again, this time in my parent's dining room. Possibly they were matchmaking, even though Dad said they were sorting out an insurance matter. Terry was still shy, still lived with his widowed father and now played golf instead of football. He invited me to partner him to a dinner dance – very popular in the 1970s – and it kind of went on from there.

The average age for marriage in those years was twenty-three for males and twenty-one for females, and here were the two of us heading for our mid-thirties. He wasn't big on candlelit dinners and hand-holding and I was willing and ready to forgo romance for the security and settledness that came with marriage, a house and family. We decided to get married, booked the church, and my mother went into a flurry of preparation.

Today I would say that the way I moved into marriage was not a good base for a relationship that the church assures us mirrors the deep, loving union of God and the church, but it was all of a piece with who and how I was at the time. What we did have in common was a

Mothering

religious faith that was deeper than words or any particular religious practices.

Terry asked his uncle, a priest, to be the celebrant at the nuptial Mass. He refused, giving my former religious life as the reason for his refusal, adding for good measure that reneging on my vows had shown me to be incapable of love.

It disturbed Terry. He told me of the conversation but we didn't go on to discuss it at any depth. We should have done so, but my husband-to-be almost never talked about emotional issues and I put up walls to protect myself from the hurt of what had been said and what might possibly be true. The wedding went ahead in our parish church and with a different celebrant. It was a joyful family occasion, imaged by a photo of a tired-out four-year-old asleep under the billiard table while my father and his brother tried to outdo each other in their speeches.

My parents had decided that they would give downsizing a go, and Terry and I bought their house. Like most couples of the era, we assumed we would fill the four bedrooms with the babies that would come. But a barely confirmed pregnancy turned out to be ectopic and then there were no more. I agonised over my failure to conceive, to understand and accept that motherhood wasn't a right that came with being a woman but a God-given gift, a gift that I felt God was withholding from me.

Friends and family were having babies, my midwife sister-in-law told us about fifteen-year-olds who were being encouraged to keep their babies, while Terry and I were in a muddle of sadness and anger wondering why God found us lacking. Infertility is as uncomfortable a word as is the process of diagnosis. Everything that is private and personal is laid out for testing and inspection, and Terry found this more humiliating than I did.

A Gentle Unfolding

In-vitro fertilisation was in its very early stages and not widely available to older couples, as we were classified at that time. Terry was what is familiarly known as a devout Catholic and would never have agreed to it anyway. Me, I would have done whatever it took to birth a child. Then, as now, I believed that God's mercy sees through to the heart of the tangle of needs, intuition and expectations that we call decision making.

One of the lovely things about Terry was his willingness to go with the flow. It seemed passive and could be infuriating to a doer like me, but it came out of a deep faith in God. Having a family was important to me, but not so much to Terry, and even though I never quite came to terms with the pain and disappointment of not birthing my own children, I caught some of Terry's way of leaving the future to God and gradually a measure of acceptance settled in me.

God's response was a gentle suggestion that maybe we could look outside the square. We decided on adoption, still an option in the 1970s, applied to Catholic Family Welfare, filled in papers, had a couple of interviews and eventually received a letter in the mail saying that our application had been refused. No reason was given and a request for one was denied as being against their policy.

Once again we picked ourselves up and I kept looking outside that mythical square. One summer afternoon I did one of those intuitive things that occasionally got me into trouble. I made a phone call to the Sisters of St Joseph explaining that my husband and I were in a position to offer a home to a child who was in need of one.

It turned out that the sisters were in the process of closing their large children's home in favour of suburban houses staffed by parent couples. Interviews and explanations followed until, one unforgettable weekend a couple of months later, three shy children, siblings in need of permanent care, came to enrich our lives and leave my

Mothering

'anything for a quiet life' husband wondering what marrying me might have got him into.

God has a sense of humour. Instead of Terry and myself eating together, chatting about our day and enjoying a glass of wine, there were three lively children, Paul, Maria and Peter, sitting around that same kitchen table, all talking at the same time and full of questions about the kind of food I was serving up. Sunday nights the children sprawled on the floor and watched family sit-coms while we mourned the loss of our preferred ABC programs.

Instead of a cuddly baby we were parenting three school-aged children, two of whom had been in care since they were little more than babies and whose former placements had failed. Alcohol was a perennial problem for their parents, both of whom had lost contact with family who may have been supportive. When the mother moved interstate, the father was not in a position to cope with a toddler, a baby and an older child, and placed the three of them in the care of the Sisters of St Joseph.

They were well looked after but they didn't thrive, whether in the orphanage or in a family group home where several children from different families were in the care of a live-in foster family. Wherever they were, in the absence of any extended family of their own they clung to one another.

God works in mysterious ways. Yes, it's a religious cliché, but it's so true. We wanted to foster, we didn't want to move out of our own house and into a group home, and the children's home had a family of three children who needed a mother and father and a house where they would be allowed to be the family that, despite their rocky beginnings, they knew they were.

Surprisingly, and in a very short time, they settled in and I gave up my part time teaching and became a full time mum. Their father

A Gentle Unfolding

visited occasionally but Terry and I became their parent figures with all that entailed.

Those early years of fostering are a blur, like a film on fast forward. There was ballet for Maria, Saturday football for Peter, scouts for Paul. We enjoyed meals that celebrated and stimulated their burgeoning taste buds, explored the countryside with weekend picnics, celebrated birthdays and went on a family holiday. For the first time in their young lives they had bedrooms where treasures could be accumulated.

My mother quickly became Nana, and with no memory of their own mother they began calling me Mum, while Terry was Pop because they already had a dad they saw occasionally. As Terry's and my birth families generously opened their hearts and homes to them, our three children began talking about aunties, uncle and cousins, all of whom were generous when birthdays and Christmas came around.

As foster parents we were assigned a social worker. Ever mildly anti-authority, I deliberately scheduled appointments with her in school hours so the children would not be home. She was a nice person and I found her helpful but I didn't want her asking the children questions that would make them feel any more different to their peers than they already felt. My instinct said that the more normal their upbringing could be the better would be their long term prospects. The Josephite sister in charge of the fostering program, not a social worker herself, noticed, smiled and said nothing. She was the one I went to when I wanted a bit of mothering myself as I struggled with difficult parenting issues and needed loving and wise encouragement.

These were 'doing' years. Like Martha, I was busy about many things, but I never lost the yearning to be Mary. I missed having personal space, time to be. Then, when it was available I found something else to do. Between marriage and mothering there was plenty to do

Mothering

and much to worry me. I had little idea that through the problems and heartaches I was learning about love, God-style. Life was trying to tell me so much that I wasn't ready or willing to learn.

10

A baby girl

Four years went by and life had become very ordinary and settled. So much so that when the Victorian Department of Human Services opened its adoption lists we felt we were in a position to apply. Group sessions, couple interviews, one-on-one interviews followed, even a nerve-racking inspection of our home and an interview with our three foster children.

My six-foot-four husband left one interview feeling, as he said, 'small enough to slide under the door'. For months he refused to go back. I worried about our now-diminished chances of adoption, about my longing for a baby, for the pain this was putting him through.

The adoption agency invited us to try again and this time we made it through the gruelling process. Kate, our adopted daughter, was born on 21 August 1978. Six weeks later we picked her up from the family who were her interim foster parents and brought her home to three highly excited children and a family hand-me-down cradle.

Our joy and the sense of completion that we all experienced lasted a little over five months. One afternoon, between school pick-up and Terry arriving home from work, Kate was admitted to hospital. I had

A baby girl

been vaguely worried that our formerly bubbly baby didn't seem to be making eye contact with any of us. More telling, seemingly overnight she developed a lump between her shoulder and her neck. The doctor made phone calls and some hours later Terry and I walked out of a large Melbourne hospital carrying the empty Moses basket between us. The specialist suspected cancer and Kate had been admitted for further tests.

During the weeks that followed I retreated behind a wall, putting on a stoic mask and trying to keep everything running smoothly in a bid to stop the pain that washed through me day and night. I don't remember praying about it or even getting angry with God. I was powerless. I hurt and I wanted it to stop.

People were more than kind and I said all the right things in response. And all the time baby Kate was suffering from the effects of the cancer treatment. She didn't recognise me and there wasn't a thing I could do about it. Six weeks after that diagnosis, Kate died during the night. I wasn't there to hold her as she went into the hands of God. We were asked and gave permission for an autopsy, which eventually told us that she had a brain tumour, probably had been born with it, and the tumour I had found had been a secondary.

Kate's death and the months that followed were the loneliest I have ever experienced. If Terry shared my grief then I wasn't aware of it. He never talked about her then or in the years that followed. Nobody did. So I grieved alone. With three children still to care for, one now in secondary school, there was plenty to keep me occupied at home. Writing for *Let's Go Together,* as well as teaching weekly RE classes in the local state school filled in the gaps and kept my real feelings at a safe distance.

The social worker assigned to us when we adopted Kate suggested that when we were ready to adopt again our request would be consid-

A Gentle Unfolding

ered favourably, as long as we were willing to accept an older child. So we gave away the pram and assorted baby equipment and returned the cradle to its rightful owners.

Nine months after Kate's death I received a telephone call that left me both laughing and crying. There was a baby, a baby girl, and the social worker said, 'I think she's perfect for your family.' Two days later we piled the three children into the car and the five of us went to make the acquaintance of this new little sister. A scramble of preparation followed, then a few days later we all went back to the interim foster parents and this time we brought home a baby.

She was seven weeks old and we called her Mary-jane. She was not, and never would be seen as, a substitute for Kate, but welcomed and loved for herself. And love her we did. She was sociable almost from the time she was born, happiest napping in a bean bag in a corner of the kitchen where life flowed loudly around her, walking at nine months in an effort to keep up with her older siblings and talking fast so she could get her bit into the conversation.

Now an adult, Mary-jane has a loving relationship with the woman who at the time of her birth was not in a position to be the kind of mother she wanted to be. This new relationship has introduced her to her three younger half-brothers and in no way takes anything away from the mother-daughter relationship between Mary-jane and myself.

If I could return to the months of Kate's illness and death, maybe I would do things differently. There must have been groups that would have encouraged me to put words around the guilt I was feeling about all the things I should have done or might have done. I could have pestered the adoption agency to let me contact Kate's birth mother, whose grief at relinquishing her child was now doubled. And I wouldn't be quite so forgiving of my parish and its priests who certainly didn't visit

A baby girl

my bereaved family. Was this because Terry's priest-uncle celebrated her requiem Mass?

There's no textbook way to grieve. Grieving is a messy, painful, confusing process. It's personal and life-changing and it never really goes away. Years later I would be part of a bereavement support team and it affirmed my personal experience that, though the flowers and cards I received after Kate's death were appreciated, I just wanted to talk about her – and nobody, in or out of my family, gave me that opportunity. Possibly that was because my body language was sending 'Do not touch' messages.

I'm an introvert and we cry on the inside. Maria, my foster daughter broke though that boundary one afternoon when she was hanging around watching me change Mary-janes's nappy. 'You know', she said, 'if Kate hadn't died we'd never have had Mary-jane.' She let the remark trail away, so matter-of-fact but full of wonder, and in that moment I experienced God's healing in the words of a child.

I was an older mum and my children were gifted to me by other mothers, so my experience of being a mother differs from that of most of my women friends. Years on, talk of pregnancies and births can still unsettle me. Even as I rejoice in my now adult children I still carry some of the pain of my infertility. Five boys, ranging in age from twenty-six to four might call me Nana, but I will look in vain for physical traits of myself or Terry in any of them. That is why I cherish the occasion when Maria, by then a mum with three boys of her own, told me that all she learnt about mothering she had learnt from me.

My own mother was a country girl who preferred the city, moved to Melbourne, became a Catholic in spite of her mother's strong opposition, married my father during the Depression, and had four children, starting with me. When I was still a teenager, at great

A Gentle Unfolding

personal cost, she gave me the freedom to follow my heart, to be myself. In a way she gave me life twice over.

I'm not really like her. She was passionate about golf, liked a game of cards, knew how to hold her tongue, and was always known to be 'a perfect lady' – which is another way of saying that I take after my father! She died suddenly nearly twenty years ago and I still miss her gentle, non-judgmental presence and regret that in my selfish, busy life I never got around to asking her all the questions for which I now want answers.

There's something mysterious, something God-like, about mothering, however it happens. I saw it years ago in those Aboriginal women in the Northern Territory. I've heard it echoed in a friend's voice as she talked of the pain she felt in not being able to protect her middle-aged son from his own impulses. I watch my career woman daughter and her friends competently and lovingly coping with toddler meltdowns and babies with reflux and I rejoice in the way they have embraced being mothers, how it rounds out their lives into something that looks to me like a sacred space.

Mothers reflect God's love and care in a multitude of ways and I believe that through my experience of mothering and being mothered I have touched God. My day-to-day expressions of parental loving and being loved reach into the very core of my being and are a living, mind-blowing model of what my relationship with God could be.

It took me years to learn that because I often lost sight of it in the full-on of my days. But in quiet moments, from giving Mary-jane her midnight feed to holding children and grandchildren in prayer, I sometimes get a glimpse of the mystery that surrounds me – that, to the children given to me to mother, I am the face of God whom we call Mother.

11
Ordinary Time

Whenever I am asked about my family I take a deep breath. Will I give the long version or will I fudge the truth and go for a conventional answer? My family is somewhat irregular and the telling becomes a little complicated. Of course there is no such thing as a normal, regular family. Families come in all kinds of shapes and sizes, none of them perfect and all of them unique.

Family might be an elastic kind of concept, but nevertheless Terry and I worked hard at being an 'ordinary family'. More than anything else I wanted our children to fit in with their peers, to experience the hands-on responsibilities and delights that go with ordinary family life, to be free to grizzle about the limits imposed by parental restrictions.

We did all the usual things, like birthday parties and holidays, started our own family traditions, encouraged better academic achievement and worried about what the future might hold for these children we called ours. We encouraged contact with their birth parents and kept discouraging social workers we considered were capable of upsetting our fragile family balance.

I needed the experience of ordinary time even more than the children. My years in the convent had left me with a swag of years

A Gentle Unfolding

that differed in nearly every respect from that of other women in my age group. When we came together to form a family, neither I nor the children had experienced either the tedium or the rewards that came with day by day living in an ordinary house in an ordinary kind of suburb. One way and another, the years up until then had institutionalised us. It left them and myself feeling different, set apart from ordinary life. I needed these years to immerse myself in domestic routine, to catch up with ordinary time and to gift them with something the same.

My years as a stay-at-home mum seesawed between life-giving and draining. I cooked, cleaned, shopped, sewed and taxied children to their various activities. I threatened to leave the three older children by the side of the road when they fought in the back seat of the car and sometimes wished someone would leave me there instead. There were days and weeks when the triviality and blandness of everyday was comforting, and parent-teacher interviews that were anything but.

The institution that is the Catholic Church tries hard to value families. The clergy who write the documents, attend the synods and write even more papers to explain things further still are seriously removed from the push and pull of everyday family life. I find it frustratingly inappropriate to be asked to take seriously documents on marriage and family that are compiled by a group of aging celibate males. I wonder what would happen if every bishop in the world took a year-long sabbatical and spent it with a family – one with toddlers and teenagers and both parents working to pay the mortgage and school fees.

One of the tactile expressions to come out of Vatican II in 1964 was 'domestic church'. The term has its origins in the early Church Fathers who grudgingly conceded that married households are the

Ordinary Time

basis of Christian community, despite their personal preference for celibate asceticism. The expression evidently appealed to Pope John Paul II because time after time he said that 'the family, in its many forms, constitutes the church in its fundamental dimension'.

I understood what purple-clad prelates were getting at when they linked domestic with church, but the ordinary years were teaching me that 'church-speak' was not always in touch with the realities of ordinary families. As I experienced it, the domestic bit was the everyday stuff that went with four children and a husband while the church was a misty background of beliefs and practices. If the church functioned as a family instead of a top-heavy bureaucracy then I could see a connection. Some years later I would read an article that spoke of our church being wrapped in families, and I thought it a more realistic way of describing the tenuous connection that exists between church and family.

Terry and I did our best to live by Gospel values. Every time we listened to a longwinded story about something that happened at school, broke up warring siblings or applied band-aids and a hug to heal a hurt, we were living out the values of Jesus, the itinerant Jewish preacher whose words still echo around the world.

The Christian way of living had been passed on to me by my parents and their parents, and back through the generations. We did our best to be a family where Jesus would feel at home, because, despite our differences and occasional dysfunctionality, it's where we experienced love.

Families are where God is first encountered and imaged – physically. Once I had the awe-full experience of seeing my unborn grandchild through the wonder that is an ultrasound scan. While the technician measured the baby's head, peered into the mouth to check for cleft palate and gently nudged him to move so that she could

A Gentle Unfolding

measure leg bones, my eyes adjusted to the shades of grey, streaked and blotched by black and white that took me into the world of the baby in the womb.

I marvelled at what I saw. A beating heart, half the size of a human thumbnail, fingers and toes, ten of each, minute kidneys, a perfect, miniature spinal cord and, delightfully, a little tongue practising sucking. The words of the psalmist floated into my mind: 'You created my inmost self, knit me together in my mother's womb. For so many marvels I thank you; a wonder am I, and all your works are wonders' (Psalm 139:13-14).

This wasn't just any baby, but someone who was already part of a family – our family. He was already fingerprinted by God, but, as Teresa of Avila said, God has no hands but ours, so he would first experience God's loving touch in his family, in the safety of arms, the back patting to relieve colic, fleeting kisses dropped on his head, tickles that produce a chuckle.

Scripture tells us that God is Love, and a baby's first experience of that love is in the touch of a parent. Take that away and the scriptural words, God is love, have no foundation in a person's physical reality. I am always moved by the pictures one sees of a baby in a humidicrib being gently stroked with just one finger. Touch lives as a memory of God in the child's soul.

Experiences of life – forgiveness, community and symbol – occur first in a family. When I was a small child and did something wrong I got a smack – not often, but it happened. My young grandsons are sent to the naughty corner, the number of minutes determined by their years. What follows is like sacramental reconciliation, family fashion – naming the offence, a promise not to repeat it, all tied up with a hug. And it happens over and over again – the Gospel in action, forgiving seven times seven. Like my ultrasound experience, family connec-

Ordinary Time

tions, however they are formed, are fingerprinted with the mystery that is God.

One by one, Paul, Maria and Peter eventually left to try life on their own. The ways they chose didn't always meet with our approval, but it was time to let them go, to trust that the values they had absorbed during their years with us would be the underpinning of their life journey. I'm not sure how their lives would stack up against a traditional Catholic measuring stick, the kind that equates Catholicity with regular attendance at Mass, but Jesus would give them top marks for the kindness and compassion they bring to their relationships and workplaces.

The church didn't invent community; it piggybacked the terminology on to every family's experience of being an entity in themselves and part of a larger group. Right through their childhood years our three foster children had always formed a tight unit within the larger one in which they lived. This has flowed over into their adult life.

I'm proud of them. Proud, too, that as well as having formed their own family units as adults they still value their childhood experiences of themselves as a distinct family, encompassed in the larger family that we called the Lynches.

12

Let's Go Together

Hanging on my bedroom wall is a framed postcard of three rooms that open out into one another, merging into a space where a woman sits reading by a window. She has retreated to a place that she can call her own while still remaining in touch with her household. It reminds me of the woman I was in my hands-on mothering years. In the midst of marriage and children, busy like Martha about many things, I never lost the yearning to be Mary.

The something that had initiated my entrance into religious life never quite went away. Sometimes I recalled those Sunday afternoons when my teenage self stretched out to touch into the God-yearning inside, and I feared I might have left her behind when I signed my exit papers. I missed having personal space, time to read or just lose myself in a reverie, but when it was available I found something else to do.

Around this time I picked up a second-hand copy of the Thomas Merton autobiography, *The Seven Storey Mountain*. In this, and in the many books that followed, Merton says over and over again that our real self, the self that God knows, is to be found in the context of our everyday. I took that on board, gave it some thought and decided that his day-to-day realities were a piece of cake compared to mine. Not for him the struggle to pay the mortgage, the contrariness of fractious adolescents, one of whom may or may not have been smoking something suspicious and another staying out past her curfew, or a husband who played golf when there were lawns to mow and guttering that needed to be cleared.

What I failed to see was that while Thomas's monastic timetable might leave lovely gaps of space for him to read, pray and reflect, it came with a get-up bell that clanged hours before sunrise three hundred and sixty-five days of the year, no holiday trips and a boring, meatless diet that rarely varied. There was nothing glamorous about a lifestyle like that: in fact it sounded tiresome – just like mine often seemed. I might have longed for something I called God, but failed to recognise God's presence in the tedium of deciding what to cook for dinner, cleaning the bathroom or trying to block out teenage music played at full volume.

The domestic ordinary had been dismissed by just about all religious hierarchies as trivial, without depth. That changed in the years following Vatican II as more women became educated theologically. They began reflecting on the sacredness of the ordinary and the ordinariness of the sacred. One frazzled woman went as far as describing her experience of finding God in the details of housework as a theology of interruption. I got what she meant when I learnt to stop and look at the world with the newness of a toddler patting a dog or the immediacy of the present moment to a hungry teenager. These were valuable moments in my life. They slowed me down, gave me space to see the sacred in what was very ordinary.

Growing respect for the riches contained in everyday things flowed over into being one of the *Let's Go Together* writing team. It gave me an outlet for my dragon woman self while my written

A Gentle Unfolding

contribution was being fuelled by my growing experience of the importance of everyday family life.

Let's Go Together was resource material for religious education classes in both government and Catholic schools in Victoria and various parts of Australia. It was a life-centered approach to education in faith in keeping with approaches instigated by the documents of Vatican II.

From as far back as 1566 to the 1960s the matter for religion classes came in a pocket-sized book called a catechism. Theological information – centred around the commandments and the sacraments – was presented in a question and answer format. Children were expected to memorise these answers. While in keeping with educational practices of the time this didn't do much to nurture faith. As approaches to how children are educated gradually changed, religious education tagged along.

During the 1960s and 70s the catechism was replaced by a whole raft of religious education material, particularly from the United States. These were very attractive hardback books with colourful pictures, lots of biblical content and a strong liturgical emphasis. But they were expensive and the language and graphics were often unfamiliar to Australian children.

The Melbourne Catholic Education Office began distributing a folded A4 weekly handout that was inexpensive enough to put into children's hands, something they could take home and share with their parents or carers. Writers like me, all with teaching background, met once a month to toss around ideas for forthcoming issues, decide on approaches and guarantee to have our written contributions back to the editor in time for photos, graphics and layout.

Let's Go Together contained deep Catholic theology wonderfully wrapped up in words that touched into experiences that were familiar and age relevant. There were puzzles, prayers and songs, ideas for dramatisation, and, my favourite, stories. We were not paid for our contributions, and didn't expect to be, but I do think that the writers should have been acknowledged by name. That never happened.

When I was asked to be on the committee who were writing new guidelines for religious education in the Melbourne archdiocese, I realised I was out of my depth. I was creative and practical but my theology was woefully inadequate and I lacked the church-speak that the task needed if it was to pass episcopal scrutiny. It was time to do something more about my personal and ongoing religious education. Mary-jane was now in pre-school, Paul and Maria were out in the big wide world, so I had some me time. I enrolled to study for a graduate diploma in religious education.

What a great time that was! In order to read the lecturers' overheads I bought a pair of glasses and even managed to hand in the necessary assignments. The lectures pushed my boundaries. Whereas previously I had read scripture from a devotional perspective, Sister Shelia Byrne introduced me to scriptural exegesis and opened up a whole new way of reading the Bible, especially the New Testament.

There were lectures with a psychological twist that enlarged my understanding of how faith develops and grows, and more about the intricacies that underlie morality and the way it is understood and taught. This was so new to me. Some lecturers triggered my interest in my Australian heritage, something that had lain dormant in me since primary school days, and I began seeing myself as an Australian Catholic, instead of a Roman Catholic.

The ordinary years were coming to an end. There were only two children at the evening meal where once there had been four. Mary-jane had started school, and I collected my certificate acknowledging that I had earned a graduate diploma in religious education. Not a big

A Gentle Unfolding

deal in academia but it gave me great satisfaction and a desire to know more.

Terry was restless and dissatisfied with his employment and hankered for a chance to follow a dream and be his own boss. We put our house up for sale, sold it and bought the general store at Hepburn Springs, a seven days a week business in a Victorian tourist destination. The area was familiar as we already owned a weekend house there. Now Terry, for maybe the one and only time in his life, had stars in his eyes, so we ignored the fact that weekending was not quite the same as earning a living there day by day. We moved into our weekender, enrolled Peter, now the only fostered child left at home, in secondary school in Ballarat, and Mary-jane in the closest Catholic school in nearby Daylesford.

We lasted a couple of years. The work was never-ending, from the early morning paper deliveries to the evening close, with little financial return for all our effort. The freehold was old and so were the fixtures and fittings. Every time something broke or stopped working we had to call in a tradie whom we could barely afford.

Paula D'Arcy, a US writer and retreat leader says, 'God comes to you disguised as your life.' It reminds me of that verse in the gospels when Jesus says, 'Behold, I stand at the door and knock.' It wasn't easy for Terry or myself to recognise anything sacred in the tiredness, the messiness and the unexpected problems that made up the ordinary of those days. But we tried. A couple of things gave us life. We became part of a parish where we made friends and Terry joined the local golf club. I prepared a small group of children for first communion and confirmation and volunteered to coordinate Renew, a diocesan small-group program that immediately stimulated my interest in parish ministry.

It was not a good time in our lives, and unbeknown to either of us Terry was probably in the early stages of motor neurone disease. It took a while but eventually we managed to sell the business, and for reasons that make no sense to me now decided to remain living in the area. Terry went back to working in insurance and I reluctantly began full time teaching in a large co-ed Catholic secondary school.

13
Church lady

For a couple of years I regularly visited a special accommodation house and as I approached the door a young woman waiting to greet me would turn and yell – no other word would do it justice – 'The church lady's here.' From an open doorway along the corridor leading to the communal lounge room a battered-looking resident would give me a beaming smile. Even though he rarely came to the little prayer time we had, he recognised the Catholic connectedness between us, regularly and proudly recalling his years as an altar boy.

Sometimes I imagine the church as a giant circle. Not far from the centre, where professional Catholics such as ordained men and professed religious gather in a tight group around the pope, is another, much bigger circle. This is the Eucharistic community – the people of different generations, birth places and opinions who gather each weekend around the altar. Other circles intersect here and there with this central Catholic community. There is the parish school, usually sharing a name with the church and accommodating many people who are part of the school community but don't join the Eucharist community. Celebrations such as baptisms, first communions, confirmations, weddings and funerals touch into the Eucharist commu-

Church lady

nity circle on the appropriate occasions. Further away, but still within the large circle, there are the men and women, like my friend in the special accommodation house, who have childhood memories of Catholic practices, who tick the RC box on census day or on hospital admission forms.

From baptism on I'd always been a church lady, even if I'd rather it had not been so loudly proclaimed. I was born into Catholicism and my pre-Vatican II religious education gave me what I assumed was a blueprint for the rest of my life, while the novitiate followed that up with a crash course in religious extras. I didn't expect it would ever be any different.

That was until I went to some Friday afternoon meetings of a group who called themselves the Movement for a Better World. In 1952, inspired by a charismatic young Jesuit, Pope Pius XII had broadcast a Proclamation for a Better World. World War II might be over, but world-wide there was unease and restlessness in religious and political structures. People had high expectations of a new world order and Pius XII saw that the rapidly spreading influences of communism or capitalism were not the answer. The church needed to move out of what he called 'religious tepidity', to embrace the Gospel message in a post-war society. The Movement for a Better World spread quickly among a generation of young women and men who wanted to make the world and the church their own.

I was then a young nun in my second year of teacher training and I went to the meeting because I was desperate to go somewhere – anywhere that was away from the convent. Once there, my conservative Catholicism felt uneasy listening to what sounded vaguely heretical. But I can still recall the little spurt of fire that jumped inside me as I listened to the young presenter talking about the need for renewal in the church and for the reform of its many outdated structures. The

A Gentle Unfolding

possibility that being Catholic might not be as straightforward as I had been led to believe would never quite go away.

Angelo Roncalli must have been imbued with the same spirit that swept the Movement for a Better World, because ten years later, as Pope John XXIII, he called a Vatican Council to renew the church's understanding of the gift of faith and to find ways of expressing that faith, ways that resonated with the modern world, while remaining true to the Gospel message.

While the Council Fathers argued back and forth and published documents whose wisdom and possibilities would lead the church into a new century and beyond, I was living on a mission in Australia's outback, far from the swirling discussions and heated arguments of Catholics in touch with church politics and processes. Eventually, our isolated little world caught up with the changes, like the Mass being celebrated in the vernacular and hymns that set feet tapping and hands clapping. Across the Catholic world, catechisms were put aside in favour of more colourful and child-friendly texts and religious orders like my own cautiously opened their shut-tight windows. Bit by bit the twentieth century was creeping, sometimes galloping, into religious customs that were more at home in a different century.

Some cynics have labelled the fifteen years that followed Vatican II as 'the silly season'. Mistakes were made, but as a lay woman it was an exciting time to be Catholic. My graduate diploma in religious education study had introduced me to liberation theology, the Latin American movement that put a Catholic emphasis on the relationship between the Gospel and the realities directing people's lives, especially those who suffer injustice. It relit the years-back flame that the Movement for a Better World had lit. I joined a small faith sharing group who gathered to test the link between our everyday lives and the Gospel. It opened me up to the a world of faith that was bigger

Church lady

than me, but always came back to what was my reality, my experience.

My reality circled around the fact that we had sold the general store, even though we continued living in the district, and we had a mortgage to pay. Back in insurance Terry spent the working week in Melbourne, returning home at the weekends and I spent the week teaching RE and a sprinkling of English in a co-ed Catholic secondary school in a nearby country town.

There is something wonderfully appealing and intensely trying about a class of adolescents – sassy girls and the boys with their unfinished faces and uphill voices. However, trying to enthuse years 8 and 9 in the religious education curriculum laid down by the diocesan authorities was an uphill battle. They were not remotely interested in studying the structure of the Old Testament. They loved stories, movies, the words of songs currently on the top 40. They loved to talk about sex and similar topics of absorbing interest to mid-teens. Just about everything else was flicked as being irrelevant to their lives, which at the time was probably true. How could I teach a unit on Eucharist to students who were currently rebelling against attending Sunday Mass with their parents, or, more truly, hadn't been since their confirmation in Grade 6 and found an hour of church-speak incredibly boring?

I don't know when is the right time to study theology or gain expertise in religious language, but I do know that it's not in mid-adolescence. I recalled Fr Bob Maguire once saying 'Religion on its own will kill you. Spirituality on its own will lead you up the garden path. You've got to have them together.' Teaching an information-centered religious education by itself was not enough, so I bribed my Year 9 students with some focused meditation time in the empty church-sized convent chapel attached to the school.

A Gentle Unfolding

They loved it, lying on the carpet, the giggles gradually easing off into silence, eyes closed and the occasional student drifting off to sleep. But, however much I wanted to integrate religious content with spirituality, there were set topics to be studied and exams to be passed, reports to be prepared for parents.

Since the early days of settlement, education had been the dominating focus of the Australian church. There was an expectation that Catholic schooling would give children a good working knowledge of Catholicity, enough to carry them into adulthood. Now, in less than twenty years, we'd been introduced to things like the psychological growth of the individual, feminism and Vatican II.

Programs like *Let's Go Together* went a long way towards addressing these changes, replacing catechetical doses of theological information with language and imagery more relevant to the young child's everyday life and psychological readiness. However, secondary schools lagged behind, subjecting religious education to the same checks and balances that applied to other subjects in the curriculum.

It was a confusing time to be a Catholic. Vatican II had told us that we, all of the baptised, were the church. How were we to become an adult church when our religious education was seen as complete at the end of secondary school? Then there were the children whose whole religious education finished at Grade 6 with the sacrament of confirmation. It was presumed that any further education in faith was peculiar to priests and nuns and a few hand-picked others.

I came to the end of those two years teaching RE deeply frustrated by a religious syllabus that didn't meet the students where they were and equally upset by what I saw as my failure as a faith educator. Maryjane was in her last year before beginning secondary school, Terry was tired of living away from home and I had begun dreaming about working at a parish level. It was time for a move.

14

Pastoral associate

As Vatican II took hold in the 1970s and 80s, more and more priests applied for laicisation and the priest shortage began to bite. This exodus of priests became an opportunity for women to move into pastoral ministry in new and different ways. Some, mostly members of women's religious orders experimenting with different forms of apostolate, were seen as a quick answer to the clergy shortage in parishes. They were employed as pastoral associates.

Pastoral associates filled in the non-sacramental gaps in parishes that had until recently been staffed by a team of priests but now were down to just one. Diocesan guidelines described pastoral associates as having a significant role within the life of a parish – working collaboratively with the parish priest in developing and shaping the mission of the parish, initiating and implementing pastoral programs and encouraging the parishioners to a deeper spiritual life as well as drawing them into roles within the parish.

Teaching religious education to teenagers hadn't been very life-giving for me, or the students either, I guess. But that experience, coupled with my participation in programs like Renew and Tomorrow's Church had sowed seeds, set me dreaming of working in a

A Gentle Unfolding

parish. My reading of Vatican II documents had gradually strengthened my confidence to know and accept that it was my God-given right to be a hands-on part of the church of my baptism. Despite its skewed perception of women, that church was the setting for the way I wanted to live out my vocation, my way to God.

During the summer holidays I answered a couple of ads for a position as a pastoral associate, but when the interviewing priest in each case realised that I was Mrs and not Sister, I was found to be unsuited for the position. Their words, not mine. I determined to give it one more try before I would reluctantly return to Year 9s for another year.

A few lines in the situations vacant column of the Saturday paper featured a large parish spread across three suburbs in need of a pastoral associate. Better still, they wanted somebody who was interested in family-based religious education. Up until this time the position had been filled by a religious sister but by 1990 nun numbers were down too and the order had no one else available. I applied and after an interview with the three resident priests, they took a collective deep breath and offered me the position, even suggesting a wage beyond a religious stipend. I drove home rejoicing.

When I told an acquaintance that I had accepted a position as a pastoral associate she looked misty eyed and murmured that it would be nice to work on a farm. I was tempted to say that I worked for the Good Shepherd but thought better of it.

In much the same way that I had worked alongside Good Samaritan sisters on the motor mission, now I was to work alongside a Brigidine sister who was responsible for pastoral care in the parish. When she left to take up a similar position in a large public hospital she was replaced by another sister, who eventually moved into full time funeral ministry in the public sector. Sister Anne came next, but within twelve months was diagnosed with cancer, dying not long

Pastoral associate

after. Then came Maria, brand new to pastoral associate ministry, a five-times mum, and a perfect fit for the parish.

Women of my mother's generation, and back beyond that, had swept and dusted the church, washed the altar linen, cleaned the heavy brass vases, changed the flowers and washed up after parish functions. They called it 'helping Father'. By the time I became a pastoral associate, women had been exposed to twenty years of women's lib, the church in Australia was full of explorations into new ministry possibilities that would be acceptable to Rome and women were ready for apostolates that were broader than volunteering for the flower roster.

No matter how great the pastoral need or how mature or experienced in the faith a woman might be, so much was out of bounds to her. Only priests could say Mass, preach, baptise and anoint, forgive sin and celebrate weddings. Feminism had assured me that I could have everything, it was my right. Not me, I thought, I'm a Catholic and Catholicism is full of no-go areas if you are a woman! Pastoral associates could still only assist the priest in the parish.

Being a woman working in church ministry is a bit like looking in to a lit house at night from the outside. It's familiarly domestic and there's something compelling about the sense of belonging that it conjures up. But ... you can never live in that house or be part of the life it encloses. Going all the way back to the church of the third century, women have been left on the outside looking in, never actually belonging fully. They have walked in the shadow of an authoritarian male leadership structure that the institutional church has canonised as tradition. American Benedictine Joan Chittester says that male religious dominance is not tradition but a long-lasting social practice that was based on bad biology and became theology as time went by.

My seventeen years as a pastoral associate were split unevenly between three different parishes, each of them with more than one Mass

A Gentle Unfolding

centre. It was a bit like being a curate crossed with a 'Father's helper'. A small group of older ladies who were regulars at morning Mass muddied the waters somewhat when they stated that they liked Sister Judith's Mass — referring to the once a week liturgy of the Word with communion that was my responsibility! They never did believe the Mrs bit.

Despite the ecclesiastical drawbacks, these were good years, a celebration of gifts that open up and flow into the church community when women and men work collaboratively in ministry. The priests were the celebrants of the sacraments, but they shared the multitude of tasks that were associated with them. I was given an almost free hand to create meaningful liturgies and occasionally presided at a graveside burial. I initiated family-based religious education programs for children who attended government schools and all the while observed church happenings as they were played out in the parish house.

I lost my church innocence one afternoon as the sexual abuse scandal hit the headlines. One of the priests in my parish team shrugged his shoulders and said words along the lines of, 'I suppose we all knew that something wasn't right, but ...' It was the *but* that did it. Years of seminary training with an emphasis on clerics supporting each other — regardless — far outweighed the rights of parents who assumed their children were safe in a religious environment.

As I heard that sentence, not only priests fell off their pedestals but my respect for the institutional church tumbled as well. I felt prickly inside and out. My passivity had been disturbed and that would be a good thing.

As more priests I had known and admired were laicised, I dithered between deep sadness that these good men were rejecting the gift of priesthood, a gift that canon law would not permit me to accept, and anger with a church who seemed unwilling to examine the way priesthood fitted into the world of today.

Pastoral associate

Canon law is very restrictive. If the ruling that the pastor or leader of each parish must be a priest could be overturned it would give qualified lay men and women and male and female deacons the authority to lead some of our faith communities. Such a ruling would have two important consequences. It would disconnect the roles of priest and pastor and begin to change the current culture of clericalism. Perhaps more significant, it would have the potential to shift the emphasis of pastoral leadership from the celebration of the Eucharist back to the preaching of the kingdom.

Once someone asked my mid-teen daughter what I did work-wise. She shrugged her shoulders and replied nonchalantly, 'She works for the church. She's religious.' I had hoped that pastoral associates would be my peer group, women like me sharing the ups and downs and creative possibilities of pastoral ministry and learning to cope with the vagaries of clerics and the institutional church. It wasn't like that. Gatherings of pastoral associates often had more the feel of a union meeting than a community experience. While I appreciated their focus on pastoral associates being entitled to a just wage and professional support in workplace disputes, what I wanted most was the friendship of a peer group.

When I was tired or disappointed about something or other I wondered why I persevered in this way of life. Teaching paid better and weekends and school holidays would have left me free to do my own thing. There would have been fewer night meetings and, more importantly, I wouldn't have been labelled 'religious', as though I walked around in an invisible clerical collar or was a nun in disguise. Maybe it was in my genes, traceable to my Methodist ancestors and their history of hands-on church involvement. The truth was, God is a seducer and like Jeremiah I let myself be seduced.

15

Faith educator

One of the parishes that employed me, St Christopher's, was in a large working class area popular with first generation Italian/Australian families and I spent nine years there as pastoral associate. It was 1990 and in the spirit of Vatican II St Christopher's was experimenting with a format known as team ministry. Leadership in the parish was shared by three priests and two pastoral associates – a religious sister and me. It was a concept that appealed to me immensely.

The house we worked in, known as the parish house, had a homely feel despite being cramped and poorly constructed. We pastoral associates were fortunate to have our own office while each of the priests made do with combined bedroom-offices. Lunch times, Monday to Friday, the team, secretarial staff, and anyone else who happened to be in the house, gathered around the large kitchen table for a meal prepared by the part time housekeeper.

Weekly team meetings were held in a funny little internal room that had originally been a courtyard. For what was a randomly chosen group of people, we got on remarkably well. The mix of temperaments and personalities made for a diversity of opinions and responses and team meetings could be sparky. We could have been described as

Faith educator

pragmatic idealists, some of us leaning more towards pragmatism than others, but our shared faith helped us to keep our eyes on the bigger picture – the body of Christ. As I think about it now it seems to me that we were a microcosm of the church that Vatican II had envisaged – women and men gathered around the Gospel, our adult faith integrated into different lifestyles, flowing out into ministry and back into everyday life.

One of the overwhelming successes of Vatican II was that it gave Catholics a renewed, dynamic vision of church in which everyone is called to put their God-given gifts into practice. I was employed to work in the area of faith development while the other pastoral associate was responsible for pastoral care. Gradually my role spilled over into areas that had formerly been seen as clerical only.

Australian parishes had begun celebrating what was known as the third rite of reconciliation, a communal liturgy that culminated with a general absolution. I was invited to write a liturgy that would be appropriate for the rite in our parish in preparation for Easter. The gathered community found it different but they liked it.

The few years that I was responsible for crafting the parish Lent and Advent reconciliation liturgies were a high point in what I was beginning to call 'my ministry'. Ministry had always been seen as a clerical word, connected with priesthood and ordination and not to be confused with the priesthood that is the birthright of every baptised Christian. Lay people were beatitude people, feeding the hungry and clothing the destitute, comforting the sick and visiting prisoners. The lines between what used to be known as the lay apostolate and sacramental and priestly ministry were becoming blurred. Ministry was no longer defined by what a person did, but instead was rooted in Gospel motivation.

Maybe, I told myself, just maybe this means that women who have

A Gentle Unfolding

experienced a call to priestly ministry might be able to answer that call.

Being given the opportunity to write reconciliation liturgies for the parish community gave me the freedom to trust my growing appreciation of the deep truths that lay hidden in the theological language that encased the sacrament of reconciliation. The theatrical part of me then translated this into colour, action, word, music and symbol, using language that was relevant, of the people. In between, there were spaces that I hoped would be reflective and prayerful, culminating in a communal absolution given by the priest. The scriptural passage on which these liturgies were based was infused and coloured by my woman's experience and Sister Marguerite's storytelling legacy.

And the people came – and came back the next year and the next. Only once did I ever suggest to the parish priest that maybe I could lead such a liturgy. The yes was grudging, hedged around with an unvoiced fear that this time I was going too far. Within a year the communal celebrations of reconciliation in parishes across Australia came to an end. It appeared that the people's appreciation of this more user-friendly acceptance of their need for forgiveness was not in line with the church's understanding of sacramental reconciliation.

It wasn't easy to let go of such an opportunity to use my gifts, giving parishioners an experience of liturgy that moved them emotionally and at the same time opening up passages of scripture from the perspective of a married woman, someone familiar with the challenges of parenting. The church hierarchy were constantly on guard against lay people, especially women, and even some clergy, getting liturgical ideas above their lowly station and lack of understanding. We saw sin and forgiveness as it happened on the ground. The church viewed it from more lofty moral heights. Until women are accepted

Faith educator

for ordination and bring their more ordinary experience to sacramental theology we will struggle to marry the two. Till then we can never be a whole people of God. At present women can walk behind, even alongside, but never out front and alone.

Then came the was RCIA.

Almost without exception, the children I taught in the Northern Territory were cradle Catholics, baptised soon after birth, as were the children who were part of the motor mission program. Adults, such as my mother, who sought to belong to the Catholic community, were called converts and were required to meet several times with a priest who took them through the theological implications and prohibitions that went with Catholicism.

Then came the Spirit wind we know as Vatican II, reminding us that baptism is more than a ritual and an excuse for a family gathering to celebrate the birth of a baby. The Vatican Council, concerned that baptism was being under-valued, turned the ecclesiastical clock back about seventeen hundred years and restored the Rite of Christian Initiation of Adults, a new-old way of approaching adult Catholic initiation, familiarly known as RCIA.

My years of involvement with RCIA spread across four different parishes and four different times. They could be summed up by the young Vietnamese woman who came to a meeting waving a New Testament and flooring me with the remark, 'I read this. I want to know what happened next.'

This method of preparing adults for baptism or to come into full communion with the Catholic Church happens in a group environment. It's not a program but a process that culminates during the Easter vigil. Its content is determined by the questions of the enquirers, their life experience, their reasons for exploring Catholic beliefs and practices. Not everyone who came looking for answers stayed.

A Gentle Unfolding

Sometimes they wanted a quick religious fix; occasionally Catholicism didn't fit their searching.

Accompanying adults in their religious searching overturned my complacency about the way I understood baptism. And having to explain matters of faith to an enquiring adult quickly picked out the holes in my understanding of the beliefs I carelessly enumerated in the creed.

Exploring what Catholics believe is pretty straightforward, but coming to grips with what that belief means in the age we live in, how it resonates in daily life and how those beliefs and practices arose from early Christians and detoured through the centuries to the present wasn't just interesting, it was exciting.

Those RCIA sessions were a wonderful melting pot of scripture, church history, prayer, Catholic terminology, theology, saints and traditions. They exposed the depths of my ignorance about my religion and sent me scurrying for information. More importantly, they helped me realise that while these enquirers were seeking practical answers to their religious questions they hungered for the spirituality that underlay them.

My one regret now that I am no longer involved in this adult faith ministry is that I didn't follow the whispering voice of the Spirit and create opportunities and possibilities to give new Catholics the support they needed and often would have appreciated in the couple of years after RCIA. For whatever reasons, and they are many, we Catholics talk fluently about community but we don't do it very well.

16

Ripples

Just as there is no one way of being family, there is no straight-up-the-middle way to educate children in faith. We live in a complex pluralist society where many belief options are offered in what some social commentators call a 'faith supermarket'. Children come to know about God through everyday experiences, but those experiences are mediated through people – in relationships, where there is love, forgiveness, discipline, security and self-esteem.

I'm passionate about parents being the educators in faith for their children but it's a tough call for most parents. They underestimate their experience of the sacred. I meet young parents, who have twelve years of Catholic education behind them. They have within them the religious truths and Gospel values that enrich their lives but they lack the language or even the opportunity to talk about them. Add to that perhaps a partner who is indifferent to religious practices or can't see what all the fuss is about – 'Let the children choose for themselves when they are adults' – and it all becomes too hard. Their children go off to the Catholic school or a Sunday morning class, to be educated in faith by someone else.

My time on motor mission had sparked an interest in finding a

A Gentle Unfolding

way to educate children in the faith, but a way that would be different, more family based. I read a lot of very attractive books that brimmed with ways to integrate Catholic practices and beliefs with family life. They fed my creativity, but when I tried them out on my family, they fell flat. Family-based religious education, Australian style, was going to be more difficult than I had assumed. Spurred on by my involvement with *Let's Go Together* and the desire to learn more about the integration of religion and life, I studied for a graduate diploma in religious education. The lectures opened doors for me that I never knew were there, introducing me to a wonderful mixture of biblical studies, church history, how faith grows and the psychological dimensions of morality. The doors were sliding doors and God was at home behind them all. When we moved to the country, I was asked to provide some ongoing religious education for a small group of teenagers. It evolved into a monthly Sunday night home-based group, with three families, parents and teens, all participating.

Three years later, in my initial interview at St Christopher's, I was asked to share my vision for a family-based religious education program that would replace the current government school classes and after-school sacramental programs. I can't remember what I said but, whatever it was, within days I had begun calling that vision Ripples. It was a user-friendly name and its theological implications were summed up in the byline: *Ripples – because the waters of baptism ripple through our lives.*

My first week in the parish was also the beginning of the school year and parents were enquiring about the beginning date for the usual mid-week RE program for children attending non-Catholic schools. My idea was to swap the once-a–week after-school lesson for a whole day in each school holidays. As a working mum I had first-hand experience of the tension around school drop off and pick

Ripples

up. I knew, too, what came second when there was a clash between junior soccer and Sunday morning religion class. And motor mission had taught me that children's interest and concentration dwindled by four o'clock in the afternoon. The suggestion was met with sighs of relief. Holiday child-minding! Great! Offers to help trickled in.

I called them rippledays and planned them as an opportunity for the children to experience their faith community in a social setting, something that the Catholic school students experienced five days a week. It was great fun and absolutely exhausting. I never slept well the night before a rippleday as I anticipated the program and wondered what I had missed. One of the priests I worked with, one with a perceptive eye, remarked once that I could organise the grand final football match complete in every detail. Well, not quite. When the umpire blew the whistle to start the game there would be no ball! He taught me to make lists, providing a visual balance for my over the top imagination, but I don't think I ever managed to spark his creativity in response.

We met in the parish hall, which gave us plenty of room for the noisy games that introduce children to one another. Parents shared their skills in craft, read stories and cooked. The children dressed up and acted out gospel stories. They learnt songs to sing at an end of the day prayer experience, preceded by a little pocket of meditation. There was an occasional hands-on tour of the church and every year the children preparing for first communion made bread from scratch and shared it with the whole group.

If God has links with publishing companies then I'll do some eternal time for copyright offences because I used material sourced from a multitude of publications for ripplepacks, the children's take-home material. In them, graded according to age, I endeavoured to integrate ordinary family experiences with sacramental theology, minus

A Gentle Unfolding

the church-speak. There was always a line or two of scripture, an opportunity for prayer, some practical recognition of family values that are deeply Christian, and occasionally a touch of church tradition. The format was designed to invite interest and input from a parent, grandparent or older sibling. Parents were extremely anxious for me to correct and mark the finished booklets, an approach that I resisted because I felt it defeated the aim of a parent taking the responsibility for their child's religious education.

Ripples, as I saw it, was neither a process nor a program as such, but a response to the faith that parents express when they present a child for baptism in the Catholic Church. The looseness of its structure was a little different to the traditional way parishes prepared children to complete the sacraments of initiation. The ripplepacks and rippledays endeavoured to integrate family experiences of water, food, drink, oil, light, darkness, wind, fire and story with scripture, prayer, sacramental images and Christian traditions.

God is mystery, and when it comes to talking about the things of God we only have the language we know best, the language of everyday. An appreciative familiarity with the ordinariness of bread, water, wine, oil are a wonderful preparation for a later, more adult understanding of sacramental symbolism. It's a shame that so much of our feel for God, our touching into God, has disappeared into intellectual church-speak.

Education in faith starts at baptism – even before. We are born with a hunger for spirituality. I would have loved to have had the time and the parish support, as well as the courage and creativity that would have been needed, to begin Ripples at baptism. The church should help parents to educate in faith, not the reverse. The church comes wrapped in families and its parents need encouragement to recognise their own faith and to pass it on in ways that suit their culture,

Ripples

their family circumstances, their creative gifts. It saddens me to say that our church is not family friendly.

Most of my working life seems to have been spent in faith education. Ripples, my family-based program was probably my favourite. It appealed enormously to both the parent and the teacher in me. However, someone once wisecracked that it enabled me to catch up with all the cutting and pasting that I missed out by not going to kindergarten.

Some years ago I wrote a hand-out for a publishing company titled *Talking with your Child about Faith*. Earlier I had put together a couple of colouring-in booklets for small children who were either being baptised themselves or had a younger sibling doing the same. Now I look at the handout and the booklets and wonder why I failed to nurture the seed they came from.

It reminds me of a story by Jesuit storyteller Fr Anthony de Mello. In my version, a woman dreamt she walked into a brand new shop in a massive shopping complex. To her surprise, she found God behind the counter. 'What do you sell here?' she asked. 'Everything your heart desires', said God. Hardly daring to believe what she was hearing, the woman decided to ask for the best things that a human being could wish for. 'For myself I want peace of mind, happiness, wisdom and freedom from fear, and I want my children and my grandchildren to be good Catholics.' God smiled. 'I think you've got me wrong, my dear. We don't sell fruits here. Only seeds.'

Ripples was one of those seeds. I hope that its hands-on kind of faith education was able to take root in a deeply personal way, the kind that remains when book knowledge has faded away or been lost. Maybe one of those rippledays will continue to ripple through the adult lives of those children and through them into the lives of their own children.

17
New beginnings

It's called following your dream – the process of willingly uprooting yourself from the security of the known and moving into an untested space or lifestyle. Abraham did it and took his whole entourage of relations and servants along with him into the desert. They, like Sarai his wife, had no choice but to follow, all because this one man had heard a voice that blocked out every other sensible notion. I'm no Abraham, but I did it too, not once but twice.

In its own way my reason for moving the hundred kilometres that lay between Melbourne and Hepburn Springs could be seen as ridiculously impractical and Abraham-like as leaving home and entering religious life years before. My father and the rest of the extended family tutted and shook their heads and muttered about risks and never learning. I listened to them and got their point, but God had called and I said yes, in spite of whatever costs and consequences might follow.

Just as I had left behind our home in Essendon to give Terry a chance to try a different lifestyle, now he did the same for me. We rented out our country home while we waited for a buyer, put the furniture into storage and moved into a borrowed house– unheated and poorly furnished – with instructions from the owner, Terry's priestly uncle, that the furniture was not to be moved around. I was in the

New beginnings

honeymoon stage of pastoral associate life and sure that all would turn out wonderfully well.

The next three years tested that belief. Our house in Hepburn Springs remained unsold for two years and three months before it found a buyer, giving us the money we needed to buy a house in Melbourne. The borrowed house was so depressing we ended up renting another more suited to our needs, but it was a drain on our limited finances. Terry was retrenched and began showing signs of the physical deterioration that would eventually be diagnosed as motor neurone disease. I became the sole bread winner and found the responsibility onerous. Even so, I never contemplated leaving the parish and finding something that paid better. I was learning that being a pastoral associate was not a job but my vocation.

All the steps along the way – vowed religious life, teaching, marriage and mothering – had led me to this point. It was like a new beginning of an old call. Prayer had always been part of my life, but it had become domesticated over the years. Now it was a hunger and I found myself longing for a slice of prayerful space and privacy at the end of a day. Instead there was cleaning and cooking and TV chatter. I felt guilty and selfish in the wanting.

To give myself some space I began to keep a journal. I bought myself a hard-backed foolscap book, so thick it took four years to fill up with the words of other people as well as my own. There were paragraphs cut from articles or newspapers, the occasional cartoon that made me laugh even as I recognised the greater truth it embodied. Once or twice I wrote a letter, never to be posted, that helped to heal the wounds left behind by a hurtful encounter.

Writing things down became a way to put words around my inner self. I had never been very comfortable identifying emotions, let alone sharing them. The word-by-word process of writing down how some-

A Gentle Unfolding

thing was affecting me was helpful for touching into myself at a level deeper than my usual throwaway response to an emotional situation. Journaling was and still is a powerful way to make real and present the intimacy between myself and God, to come to realisations about God, myself and life.

Pastoral associates need organisational skills, energy and creativity and, above all, the ability to work collaboratively in a team. Doing ministry, coupled with family responsibilities, left me little time or energy for personal prayer and reflection. I wanted to find new ways of being me. To God I was Judith, not Mum or Mrs Lynch, Terry's wife, Mike's sister, aunty Jude or even the Sister Mary Andrina of my years in religious life – though the elderly black-clad and head-scarved women of the parish insisted on calling me Sister right up to the day I left.

When Vatican II had begun rolling out its message – *We are church: what if we meant it?* – faith sharing groups were a new and popular way for ordinary people to put words around the way their spirituality and religion plaited together. These small group programs had been sufficient to nourish my spirituality during the 1980s but now I wanted to deepen that experience of being church.

Being a pastoral associate gave me opportunities to do so by participating in some of the many programs that cluttered the Melbourne church calendars at this time. With the generous financial support of the parish, I attended a whole raft of church-centred programs and gatherings. Some were a week long, others a weekend, while occasionally there was an evening or afternoon lecture by a visiting scholar or church dignitary, but all were focused on some aspect of discipleship and personal growth.

'Effectiveness Training for Clergy and Church Leaders' gave me practical pointers about group structures and management that I still

New beginnings

find relevant. 'Re-Membering Church' fleshed out the dynamics of ministry to those who have been estranged from the practice of Catholicity and wish to return. That weekend stands out in my mind, not so much for the practices and experiences it promoted, but for the depth of sharing among the participants I experienced in the one-on-ones – like a cold drink of water on a hot day.

As preparation for the Year of the Family, I attended workshops brimming with practical ways to enthuse parents to participate in yet another *Year of*... Later that year I received a rainbow pin giving me the go-ahead to present the grief and loss program designed for children and familiarly known as Rainbows.

After a series of diocesan lectures, I received official registration as a lay minister of funerals, a ministry I liked but was rarely called upon to practice. Most Catholics, especially those who had limited contact with church, found it inappropriate and preferred a priest, a position that seemed to be shared by parish priests and funeral homes. When one of our ministry team spoke highly about a program called 'Spiritual Leaders' she had completed twelve months earlier, it lit a spark in me. The name appealed. My two years in the parish had shown me that there was nothing either/or about committed ministry. I also knew that it could be very easy to fall into the trap of defining myself by what I did, not by the way God had dreamed me into being. As a woman who was seen to be church I needed to stay in touch with God as well as having the confidence to lead, when I had always followed.

For the next twelve months, I was one of a group of ten women and men all of whom worked in church ministry. One morning a week we met at Heart of Life Spirituality Centre in a leafy Melbourne suburb. There the program leaders, a Presentation sister and a Passionist priest, guided, encouraged, and sometimes pushed us to develop spiritually and personally.

A Gentle Unfolding

Religious life had impressed on me that the self is not to be trusted, and for years I'd hidden behind that wacky reasoning. It meant that I lacked the self-awareness to recognise the strengths and weaknesses that were holding me back from being true to myself and to God's call. The Spiritual Leaders program required me to come up with goals that would address just that issue – ministry goals as well as personal goals that related to my spiritual development.

I'd always made shopping list notes for the whats and whens of my life, but having to present a succinct summary of my learning goals for this course made me cringingly aware that I'd done nothing so formal since I completed my teaching course. I panicked, wrote some notes, then tore them up. It had been pointed out to me that they were vague and 'out there', all about helping others to be Gospel people, quite missing the point that it was me who needed to be the Gospel person.

After a week of thinking about it, I sticky-taped the page together and wrote a new set of goals on the back. They said simply that I wanted to integrate my being with my doing, that I wanted to minister to others without losing sight of my individuality, and, tellingly, that I wanted to be able to articulate this to myself and others.

That was in 1993. I'm still working on the first goal while the other two are slowly becoming part of my ongoing ministry.

18

Spiritual Director

The twelve month spiritual leadership course had introduced me to John of the Cross, a man who lived three hundred years earlier. He said a lot of wonderful things very poetically, many of which went right over my head. But his words about life being seen as God in disguise had taken root in me. I knew enough about John to know that he was no stranger to a life that went slant-wise more often than not. The simplicity of that sentence and the assurance behind it gave me heart as I tried to integrate my God-relationship with the on-and-off messiness and chaos of everyday. If I was to be serious about my spiritual life then I could probably do with a bit of help. I decided to talk to a spiritual director.

I was used to thinking of spiritual direction as something for, well, other people – holy men and women, not an ordinary woman like me. My first and only experience of a kind of spiritual direction had been in the novitiate when I had to write a daily account of my morning meditation and drop it on the novice mistress's desk. She'd return it with a tick, a comment if I was lucky, and sometimes schedule a one-on-one to talk about what I had written. Forty years would pass before I had another experience of spiritual direction, and it would be very different.

A Gentle Unfolding

Meeting with the priest I chose to be my spiritual director helped me to begin the long, never-ending process of bringing my heart and head together. As a descendant of a feisty Irish great-grandmother, I don't take kindly to direction from anybody, so my spiritual director didn't have an easy job. I was adept at blocking out what I didn't want to talk about. I'd park a block away from his house and consider turning around and going home, anything to keep my inner self to myself. But deep down I knew that when I did that I kept God out too.

Slowly, we both persevered. I kept turning up and he listened to me, encouraged me to listen to my inner self and, most importantly, to name and value what I found there. The monthly meetings with him helped put me in touch with the desires and longings that swirled around my head. Patiently and gently, and occasionally challengingly, he guided me in my search for a more meaningful relationship with God.

In the months after the Spiritual Leader's course finished I had become increasingly aware of a desire to help others, ordinary people like myself, to recognise and develop their spirituality, to name the experience of God that their everyday held. My ministry team leader, not famous for thinking outside conventional squares, suggested that I 'do' theology at the Yarra Theological Union. I declined, giving as my reason that I had no wish to follow a clerical path when there was no possibility of moving on to ordination. I suppose it was my way of rebelling against church rules that cut women out of sacramental ministry. At a reflective level I was also a little fearful of my really alive faith being documented, de-heresied and written into neat, logical essays. I was still the woman whose individualistic take on religion had led to a fail in RE during teacher training!

At a fairly deep level – somewhere I didn't want to go – it looked as though God was suggesting that I explore this ministry of spiritual direction. My response was a decided 'No way.' In a swirl of push/pull

Spiritual Director

feelings, I enrolled in a weekend seminar to explore Siloam, a program that trained spiritual directors. To my relief I discovered that the tuition fee of the year-long full time program put it out of my reach. Half jokingly I told the coordinator that I would need to be backed by a religious order or married to a rich man if I was ever to be accepted for Siloam.

Nearly a year later that same coordinator contacted me with the news that the Siloam program was being revamped and would be offering a part time option, spread across two years. Would I be interested? In spite of myself, I was. I talked it over with the leader of the parish team. He discussed it with the parish financial person and the parish generously offered to split the fees with me. This meant I could just about manage financially. A little reluctantly I followed the Spirit, and enrolled in the Siloam program at Heart of Life.

I was one of a group of eight, seven of them women. Twice a week we attended lectures on subjects such as the psychological aspects of spiritual direction, the discernment of spirits, the human and religious experience of God, the experience of conversion and ethics for spiritual directors. Before we were let loose on real-life directees we participated in weekly formal practice sessions of spiritual direction, taking turns to be director and directee. Regular written assignments were expected to mirror the goals we had set ourselves at the beginning of the course as well as brim with personal experience.

Through all this I felt a fraud, that God had got me mixed up with someone else, another woman who would breeze through such a program, might even love it. I wanted to give up even though I was deeply aware that this was where God was calling me. On Siloam days I'd wake feeling like the C. S. Lewis character Aslan the lion, lying bound with ropes, surrounded by jeering little monsters flourishing scissors as they cut off the mane that distinguished him.

A Gentle Unfolding

The deeply personal interactions that were a large part of the training process, left me feeling exposed, shorn of a lifetime of self-perception that didn't match the self I kept under lock and key. The surprise of Siloam was the struggle to own the good things about myself. Pious teachings about humility coupled with a familial mistrust of affirmation had prevented me from recognising my giftedness. I hated and feared the probing questions of the Siloam leaders and my peers, didn't know how to accept the remarks that showed me a picture of myself that I didn't want to see.

But I persevered, and while it didn't get a whole lot better I did learn to recognise and name my emotions, to appreciate my God-relationship and to recognise and respect that in others. Some time in my second year of Siloam I was even able to say that I was studying spiritual direction and not feel a fraud. I accepted that it had been gifted to me by God and that even though I often wanted to give it back to the Giver, I also wanted to keep it.

As I became more tuned in to what was moving inside me, I experienced some uneasiness about the model of spiritual direction taught and practised at Heart of Life. It reminded me that years back I had questioned the motor mission format and I rebuked myself for once again trying to run before I could walk. I did my best to put my questions behind me. Underneath I was fearful that by following the way I had been taught I'd lose the 'me' approach – that as a spiritual director I'd be swallowed up by the professional dynamic and not able to move at a slower, somehow more personal pace that took into account the ordinariness of everyday family life.

This inner perception was strengthened by some time I spent with a young woman, a mother of four, soon to be five. The encounter was one woman sharing her faith with another but it had a warmth about it that I hadn't experienced in other similar but more formal interactions.

Spiritual Director

I listened, laughed, marvelled as she told her story. I didn't probe, just let the story flow. It all seemed miles away from verbatim material of spiritual direction, where the emphasis was on picking up the salient points and exploring them further. This interaction was a simple companioning in the journey of faith. It had a rightness about it. I mightn't have the more advanced skills or talents that I had recognised in some of my peers, but paradoxically my greatest resource was myself.

Siloam had begun the process that taught me about inward listening, to hear beyond the spoken word. Gradually it would become second nature to listen to my emotions and the messages my body sent me, to accept the vulnerabilities that I recognised in myself and saw mirrored in others. My contemplative approach brought with it a depth and flavour that found its unseen way into the ordinary and everyday.

In 1996, after two years of intense preparation, I received my certificate in spiritual direction and returned to full time parish ministry. For the next a couple of years I tried pre-booked, one-on-one encounters with a directee, but clients were hard to come by. In true Judith fashion I blamed myself, my lack of skill and so on. The women and men in the parish where I worked equated formal spiritual direction with professional psychology, something they vaguely mistrusted and couldn't afford anyway.

Ever so slowly I learned to trust my intuition that spiritual direction was broader than the one model I had learnt. I was still on the cusp of learning that an approach that came from both my head and my heart was probably right for me but I had no idea how to put it into practice. Eventually I would discover ways to use the skills and talents I'd been so sure that I didn't have. Only then would I be open to hear the small still voice of God and be ready to open up the gift that was Siloam.

19

Tarella space

I'm a fourth generation Australian with Irish and English ancestry, and I grew up in the city. Every time I round a particular bend in the highway linking Melbourne and Ballarat and see the high rise buildings of the city silhouetted against the sky, I get a sense of homecoming. But deep down it's the pull of the vast paddocks and endless horizons of the Mallee landscape where my mother was born that draws me. While some people gravitate to mountains and others to the sea and many feel uneasy away from the sounds and sights of the city, it's the wide open spaces of the Australian landscape that backdrops my religious and spiritual journey.

It wasn't till I did Siloam that I began to recognise the hold that empty spaces had on me. One long weekend, Terry and I took our children to visit my aunt in the little country town of Rainbow. Caught up as I was in the demands of marriage and mothering, I had blotted out my experience of wide open spaces. Even the twelve years in Australia's Top End had all but faded away. That weekend I realised that I liked paddocks that were so big that the details got lost. For the first time it made sense to me why I was comfortable with 'big pictures' and wasn't a details person.

Driving home, as the road unrolled past acres of wheat and sheep

Tarella space

land, I watched the sunset and recaptured the feelings of stillness and distance that had seduced me as a child. The stillness was alive and the distance was not the distance of alienation, withdrawal or avoidance but an awe-filled experience that spoke of God. I wondered if it was a genetic thing, that my way of looking at life was mirrored by the country that my ancestors had farmed in the more than one hundred years since my grandmother Florence Perkins, along with her parents and brothers and sisters, had travelled overland from South Australia to Victoria, lured by the availability of vast tracts of land that bordered the Little Desert.

Maybe they too had felt the pull of that landscape, a feeling of completion, a deep sense of belonging to the land. They were joined by others and a tiny farming community known as Werrap took shape. Among these pioneers patiently coaxing wheat out of the land was Charles Helyar, the young man who would become my grandfather.

In the manner of such stories, Florence married Charles and the young couple set up house. As their family increased they moved into a newly-built home, for unknown reasons known as Tarella. It was a square building with thick pug walls, a central front door, matching windows and a veranda all around. It became home to ten children, among them my mother. This simple house was set in an oasis of scrubby gum trees that opened out into vast paddocks. Over years, helped along by the times when it didn't rain enough, hills and dunes of sand blown in from the not-so-distant desert began edging into the paddocks. As a child I looked upon them as a wonderful sandy playground.

This was where my mother grew up, was educated to Merit level at the tiny one-teacher school and completed her education with a correspondence course in business management. According to family stories, she loved tennis more than more farming. Deciding that

A Gentle Unfolding

being a farmer's wife was not the life for her she defied her mother's expectations for her future, moved to Melbourne and never lived at Tarella again.

However, she did visit, especially after I was born. During my childhood the Christmas holidays were always marked by a visit to my widowed grandmother, now living in the little town of Rainbow, a township that had grown up a few miles from the early wheat farms. Once the city was left behind, the road from Melbourne was long and straight, edging paddocks laced with solitary gum trees and fences that stretched in unbroken lines as far as my young eyes could see. My brothers and I jostled for the first glimpse of the tips of the silos that would mark the end of our journey. This was my country, and, without knowing why, it felt just right. Like the Aboriginal people, I too had my Dreaming.

As a teenager, I would borrow my aunt's bike and ride out as far as the town reservoir. It was always hot and the silence was so deep and thick I felt I could spoon it up. In the silence and space I felt like I was just Judith and it felt right. Without knowing why, it reminded me of God. Apart from a crow or two cawing into the heat, the space all around me was empty, and the dreamer in me both loved that and wanted to pedal away from it as quickly as possible.

No visit to Rainbow was complete without a trip to the Tarella house where my one of uncles lived alone. I marvelled at the shearing shed with its single step up, so very high to a toddler. I peered fearfully down into the cellar, keeping an eye open for the snakes that were said to nest there. The shaded area between the house and the shed held memories of the day when my grandmother told me told me how to catch a hen, then treacherously laughed at me as I ran around trying to throw salt on its tail. Years later I would recall this space as the setting of my first experience of vulnerability.

Tarella space

Places become part of us and we become part of them. During my years as a pastoral associate I noticed how families returned to a particular church to celebrate baptisms, weddings and funerals, back to the place where they or their parents were baptised or 'all our family gets married there'. In solemn or celebratory times they tap into a need to feel that they are somewhere where they feel they belong. Such a space can be a refuge and sanctuary in time of spiritual need.

Working in a parish had introduced me to many people, but it was in casual conversations with women who were active in pastoral ministries such as RCIA, marriage preparation, lectors and special ministers, who told me that they longed for more ways to understand and express their spirituality. They were faithful to Sunday Mass but it wasn't enough. I offered the only thing I knew – spiritual direction.

Personal spiritual direction had given me the time and space to hear the God story that hides within the ordinary of my life. It kept sending me back to my Mallee ancestral roots. There was nothing very distinctive about it, except the fact that it was mine and unique to me. Memories of the silence and space I had found in the Mallee and later in the Northern Territory had allowed me to expand my personal horizons and move more deeply into the wider, spiritual dimensions of life. I wanted to give other women the same opportunity.

The ministry of a spiritual director is to listen to stories, to find the God that hides in those stories. I listened to mine and that led me to an unexpected decision. The house we lived in was built on a sloping block with unused space downstairs, I decided to set it up as a quiet space and I called it Tarella. It was more of an idea than a space. Tarella Spirituality, my spirituality website, was not yet birthed but I knew it would be a setting where women, and maybe some men, would be encouraged and supported to create pockets of silence in their own lives, to find the God-depths that lay hidden there.

A Gentle Unfolding

It had taken me such a long time to call myself a spiritual director without feeling a phony, to know what to do with this gift I had been given. When Siloam had come to an end I could sum up in three words my three main learnings from those years of preparing to be a spiritual director – silence, space and ordinary. I had learnt to appreciate and value silence, to understand that when I could shut off the chattering voices of my mind, even momentarily, the space they left behind was God shaped. I now understood that silence needs space, and that space can be a friendly place. It can be as simple as an early morning cup of tea or weeding a garden bed or just sitting in a silent house. God spaces are not confined between church walls. The spaces where we let God in have an intimacy that is deeper than words, where understanding and being in control doesn't seem quite so important.

The model of spiritual direction that Siloam had given me was a good structure, somewhere to speak about the God questions and experiences that don't fit easily, if at all, into everyday conversation. Many Australians are quietly spiritual and enjoy contemplative activities such as bushwalking, surfing, gardening, fishing, but they don't see any reason to talk about this and feel quite uncomfortable bringing God into it.

I delight in using the vocabulary of landscape, recognising how the red heart of Uluru, crumpled brown earth, now-and-again rivers and lots of gum trees have shaped and given meaning to the way I relate to God. I wanted to bring the openness of the Australian landscape to my ministry of spiritual direction, into whatever unexpected places and spaces it might take me or I might take it.

In open space there is freedom and visibility. And there is vulnerability too. There's been plenty of that in the twenty years since I created Tarella Spirituality. In her book *There is a Season*, Joan Chittister quotes an Arab proverb that appropriately describes the

Tarella space

vocation of the great-grand-daughter of a farming family: 'Every morning I turn my face to the wind and scatter my seed. It is not difficult to scatter seeds but it takes courage to go on facing the wind.'

I have spent years sowing seed. There have been one-on-ones, formal and informal, when someone, usually a woman, feels the need to talk about how they and God are coping with life. Sometimes these are at my home, sometimes at a coffee shop, now and again in the middle of a shopping centre.

I've come to understand that spiritual direction is more aptly called spiritual companioning. The teacher in me is comfortable with small groups so I've run seminars on topics as wide apart as Australian Spirituality and Women in Scripture. There have been parish prayer groups to introduce women to adult prayer, prayer days and Lenten scripture groups, reflection days. There have been monthly Sophia Circles because when women gather they tell stories. Once women know that their story will be heard and valued for itself, this more contemplative approach gives them the confidence to touch into the person they know is within them, the one with God's imprint stamped on it.

Sometimes I have been paid , sometimes not. Always I have been privileged to hear many deeply personal stories, stories that have been hidden deep inside the person, needing to be heard, to be seen as precious, to tentatively find their God connection. When I have been tempted to look for results, to believe that my efforts are all a mistake, then something happens – a chance meeting tells me of words or an image from some long-gone encounter that still echoes in someone's life and I say, 'Thanks, God. I needed that.'

Like my grandfather, who planted his wheat crop despite the possibility of drought, mouse plague or fire, I keep planting Tarella seeds.

20
About Terry

My husband, Terence George Lynch, died 11 October 1998. He was sixty-one and he died of motor neurone disease, commonly known in Australia as MND. Seventeen months earlier a specialist had reluctantly named this as the likely cause of his increasing physical weakness. We walked slowly out of the doctor's rooms into a Saturday afternoon quiet. Now it had been named we knew what lay ahead. Seven years earlier, Terry's youngest sister had received the same diagnosis.

Motor neurone disease is the name given to a disease in which the nerve cells controlling the muscles that enable us to move, speak, breathe and swallow gradually degenerate and die. It can be familial and currently there is no cure. In the months that followed his diagnosis Terry experienced increasing weakness in his legs and hands, eventually being confined to a wheelchair. His speech slurred until it became incomprehensible and swallowing difficulties meant that his food had to be pureed. This man, the height and build of a football player, gradually lost all muscle tone as the weight dropped off his bones.

In the days that followed Terry's diagnosis I experienced a deep inner stillness – a kind of shell shock. Now and again I would feel

About Terry

energised; the not-knowing was over and I would do whatever was needed to ease the future for him. Then once again grief at what lay ahead would brush its finger across my day and I found myself trying to put shape and words around all that now couldn't be and hadn't ever been.

Our marriage had not been easy, and sometimes the frustration, anger and restlessness that I had experienced over the years threatened to overwhelm me. Now I knew, without a doubt, that the past was just that, past. I had a recurring image of a massive gum tree, once tall and beautiful, now lying in the corner of a paddock, its ghostly branches stripped of leaves, reduced to its bare structure. Sometimes the tree was Terry. Other times it seemed more like our relationship.

Terry, never one to put words around his inner feelings, took refuge in action. Remembering their sister's gradual deterioration through MND, Frances, his remaining sister, suggested that he fulfil a long-time wish and accompany her to Ireland while he was still mobile. I too had been thinking along the lines of a holiday, but for just the two of us, a couple of weeks somewhere in a setting that might have made it easier for us to talk and maybe mend some of the broken fences in our relationship. Not an expensive overseas holiday. In the twelve months leading up to his diagnosis Terry had not been regularly employed and we had little money to spare.

Terry's uncle, as well as Frances and her Irish-born husband, all vetoed me, declaring me selfish and standing in his way, and off the three of them went to Ireland. Maybe I was being selfish, but I had some idea of the difficult time that lay ahead, for me as well as Terry, and would have appreciated a week or two that I hoped would provide memories of a peaceful and loving time spent together. The decision he made to accompany his family to Ireland instead pained me then, and its memory still does today.

A Gentle Unfolding

Terry walked onto the plane that took him to Ireland, but came back a month later leaning heavily on a walking stick. Over the next sixteen months his condition gradually deteriorated. When our current house no longer suited Terry's needs we sold it and bought another, this time with a wonderfully big walk-in shower and passageways broad enough to accommodate a wheelchair. Mary-jane's needs were put to one side even though she was in her last year of school, and our three foster children, who all lived in Canberra, were too far away to help. I needed help.

There was no cure, no course of treatment that would alleviate MND symptoms or give patients some remission time, but there was Bethlehem hospital. Bethlehem was the go-to place for patients and families struggling with motor neurone. As Terry's condition worsened, he would be admitted to Bethlehem for a few days, giving Mary-jane some time to be a teenager and my ever-dicey back a chance to recover, however briefly, from the constant awkward heavy lifting. My parish team was wonderfully supportive, letting me work from home whenever it was appropriate instead of from the parish house. And there was the group I named Terry's carers, and its subgroup, Terry's girls.

Friends and family had offered to help with Terry's care so I took them at their word and, teacher-wise, drew up a roster. Every afternoon one of them came to spend some time with him. Some talked sport, a couple played cards, others talked family stuff and so on. As it became necessary the Bethlehem staff lent us specialised equipment such as an electric bed hoist and a motorised wheelchair, and trained the whole care group how to use them.

Terry's girls were a zany group of women from the parish where I worked, all blessed with an approach to life that I envied but was far too serious to emulate. Terry loved them. They made him laugh,

About Terry

something I had lost the energy to do. They told him outrageous jokes and did things like visiting him when he was in respite care and decorating his hospital room with the red and black of his beloved football team, Essendon, and a life-size cutout of James Hird. Whole books are written about care and compassion and the works of mercy. Terry's carers, both the volunteers and the professional, were the words in those books.

In all the long months of his dying Terry never complained. I preach about finding God in the ordinary of life. Terry lived it, every hour and every day. He died in Bethlehem hospital from the complications of pneumonia a few weeks after our silver wedding anniversary.

Those twenty-five years contained the story of a marriage, and the days in that marriage were full of ordinary events like family celebrations, weekend picnics and the children's school commitments – and golf on Saturday. Terry was a committed member of the Knights of the Southern Cross and though the feminist me was both amused and scornful of this males-only organisation I enjoyed the social events that came with it. The challenges and frustrations of our marriage got papered over in the busyness of ordinary things

Rainer Maria Rilke, the famous German poet who died in 1926, once said: 'For one human being to love another, that is perhaps the most difficult of all our tasks, the ultimate, the last test and proof, the work for which all other work is but preparation.' If loving was an exam subject my report card would read: *Could do better.*

For different reasons both Terry and myself missed out on that preparation. Living as a religious from the age of sixteen to thirty-two, I had no experience of laying down the foundations of adult relationships and the intimacy that flows out of them and often lasts a lifetime. Personal relationships were then known as 'particular friendships' and were strongly discouraged in religious life. That loss

A Gentle Unfolding

dogged me through the years of marriage and has continued on into the loneliness of being widowed.

Terry came from a silent kind of family. His mother, who might have balanced his father's silence, was ill for many years and died when her four children were all still teenagers. His two sisters, both younger than him, joined the Sisters of Charity in their mid-teens, and his older brother married, leaving Terry and his father together – two silent men. What drew Terry and me together? It was mostly ticking clocks – in 1970 the average age for couples to marry was twenty-two for men and twelve months younger for women. We were looked upon as positively geriatric. We had met occasionally when I was in my last year of school, then sixteen years later in my parent's dining room. As the saying goes, we dated and kind of drifted into marriage.

In hindsight, what was lacking in our marriage was intimacy. Not physical intimacy, but the kind of intimacy that talks about everything, the intimacy that risks the vulnerability demanded by self-disclosure. My early adult years, coupled with a family background that wasn't into sharing feelings, had left their mark on me. Just after leaving religious life I did meet a man I loved but I didn't know what to do with this strange feeling. That relationship, originally full of promise, fizzled out and its ending grieved me.

As the years went by I realised that vulnerable intimacy is the swinging gate between human and divine love. While I had no doubt that Terry loved me, right up to the day he died, I regret that loving wasn't so simple for me. It was only after we were married that I realised it was a mother's love he craved. I wanted our relationship to be reciprocal, filled with a desire to understand the other, to appreciate each other's weaknesses and fears, to share the inevitable pain. He couldn't do that. I was left with a feeling of guilt about a marriage that didn't seem to live up to the theology of the sacrament.

About Terry

The theology of marriage reads quite beautifully, if somewhat obscurely, but it skips over all that is imposed on us the by the realities of cultures, differing temperaments and unreal expectations the media does its best to impose on us. I understood that human love mirrors God's love, that our sometimes painful revealing of our deepest self to another is matched in God's self-disclosure of God's self to us. It's like doing the tango – it takes two, moving in sync and fuelled by passion.

I believed in the sacramentality of our marriage. Despite our differing ideas of what love was or could be, we had a loving marriage. If he was ever aware of the walls I built around myself during those years in a bid not to be smothered by his neediness, he respected them, even when he was hurt. In some obscure way he was even proud of the way my life had developed. He never did understand the children when they were adolescent but he never stopped loving them, just left the discipline to me.

It's probably true to say that marriage taught me more about love than I would have learnt if I had stayed in religious life. Film, music, fiction, magazines and teenage girls talk about falling in love as not just romantic but a right, a neverending story. That is until life teaches them that there is nothing romantic about falling.

As my marriage unfolded through months and years, my falls away from true loving were frequent and painful. Time and time again I was forced to recognise that I wasn't very good at loving. I wanted the loving to be on my terms and, when it wasn't, I was very unhappy. Rightly or wrongly I envied others whom I saw as being in loving relationships. I was learning the hard way that married love is deep and true and unselfish. Just like God's love for us.

The Christmas before Terry died, Mary-jane gave us a set of wind chimes which we hung on the side veranda facing the neighbouring

A Gentle Unfolding

house. The owners complained that the chimes kept them awake on windy nights, so every evening after that I would tie them up. Now those chimes hang on the veranda of my current house. They remind me of a loving man who loved me, even when I didn't love back the way he wanted to be loved, who never complained, never turned away from God and what God asked of him, even when, nerve-ending by nerve-ending, he was silenced as effectively as those tied-up wind chimes.

21

Country lady

The grieving starts early when you are caring for someone with a terminal disease, so by the time Terry died my main feeling was relief that it was over, that Terry didn't have to wake each day to the loss and lack of dignity of MND. The plaque on the rock that surmounts his grave reads: *He lived justly, loved tenderly and walked humbly with his God.*

I was a widow and free to become me again – whoever that me might be. I went away for a few days, took time out to sit with my new way of being, to listen for the voice of God and wondered what came next. Spiritually, I felt like a fish swimming in the shallows, longing to dive into a world that lay beneath the surface, but held back by a deep powerlessness Physically, I was worn out.

Wise voices had advised me not to make any changes during the first year after a bereavement and I listened to them and continued working at St Christopher's while Mary-jane passed on a university place in favour of a twelve month work placement. But the flavour had gone out my ministry, and towards the end of the year I resigned my position as a pastoral associate, sold the house, bought another in a country town one hundred and forty-five kilometres away and set Mary-jane up in a flat near her work.

A Gentle Unfolding

The decisions weren't easy. I would miss the parish community, their easy friendship, the way they lived out their faith and their acceptance of a ministry model that was a little different. Church-wise they had gifted me with much that I would carry into whatever the future held for me. For nine years I'd been part of the St Christopher's parish team and the experience had been life-giving and satisfying. Now I was choosing to leave all that behind and replace it with – nothing fixed. No employment prospects, a house in an unfamiliar area a couple of hours away from family and friends, days to fill and basic computer skills to master with no parish secretary to hold my hand while I learnt. It was daunting – and it was exhilarating. I was farewelled during a Sunday Mass followed by a parish barbecue and presented with a giant-size card filled with messages of farewell and the gift of my very own photocopier. And then it was over.

I had begun my pastoral associate ministry in 1991 with a great deal of enthusiasm. In 1996 something happened that gave me reason to do a bit of cloud walking, to dream a little of what could be. The parish team leader, one of the two remaining priests in what had originally been a three-priest parish, planned to spend two months at a language school in Italy. Around that same time Frank Little, the Archbishop of Melbourne, had approved the appointment of a pastoral leader for the bayside parish of Aspendale.

This was something new – a married layman running the parish, preaching and conducting funerals. In fact doing everything a normal parish priest would do except the sacramental things like saying Mass, performing baptisms and hearing confessions, all of which were picked up by a visiting priest. Our team liked the idea – thought it might be something we could try for the two months the parish priest was away. We did what creative ministry teams do – we set it in

Country lady

motion. Off went a letter to the archbishop suggesting that I be appointed pastoral leader for the two months the team leader was away, leaving the second priest, a man of uncertain health, to be the sacramental minister.

Ten days later the response came —a yes and a no. In church-speak we were told that the role of pastoral leader had been established as an ecclesiastical office and my role would not fulfil the requirements of that office. What we were suggesting was not a permanent role like the one at Aspendale, but an eight-week fill-in during which the parish priest would still be the parish priest even though he was 12,000 kilometres away. However, I would be permitted to assume day-to-day pastoral responsibility for the parish during those two months and the local bishop or dean would be available for support and advice if needed. This tied it up neatly in canon law requirements. Either the bishop or the dean would fill the role of canonical administrator while I was the pastoral leader of a parish in fact but not in name. The title was immaterial and the parish went on as usual, giving me no reason to pick up the offer of advice.

During those two months, I thought a lot about what an experience like this could mean for the future of the church in Australia. Maybe the time was coming when women could be seen as the face of the church, able to provide spiritual, pastoral and organisational leadership as well as non-sacramental liturgies, especially in country towns too small for a resident priest.

Four years later, that cloud-walking dream and others like it had been shattered by ecclesiastical decisions to import priests from around the world to fill the gaps in Australian parishes. I was still grieving Terry's death and I was tired, particularly of a church that wouldn't recognise women's gifts for ministry, that assumed that a priestly vocation was linked to the male sex, that women needed

A Gentle Unfolding

to know their place and keep it. I left St Christopher's thinking my pastoral associate years were over, dreaming of earning a living offering spiritual direction and retreats to the people of country Victoria. That, of course, was another bit of cloud-walking.

I moved into my new home in Waubra, a blink-and-you're-through-it dot half an hour from the regional city of Ballarat, revved up by a misty dream of living a simple life. I'd forgotten my mother's advice given many years before: 'Darling, never live in a country town.' She knew: she was born in one. I discovered the hard way that it's not easy to become known and trusted in a country town, even one as large as Ballarat.

Month followed month and my savings dwindled while I tried to set myself up as a spiritual director. I was either not needed or not wanted, so somewhat reluctantly I began scanning the diocesan pages for a pastoral associate position. By November my simple-living idealism was beginning to be a bit too simple. When I was offered a part time position as pastoral associate in St Alipius' parish, Ballarat, I gratefully accepted.

The dreams I had at that time were not God's dreams for me and it had taken me months to accept that my ministry was still to be found in a parish. Greg was my new employer and we hit it off from the beginning. As they say, I got my mojo back. Only to lose it again a few months later when Greg was moved on and replaced by a new parish priest.

It was not unknown for an incoming parish priest to make sweeping changes cancelling programs already set up and even terminating the employment of a pastoral associate. That didn't happen and I continued working with sacramental programs. rippledays, baptismal preparation and RCIA. But it was different. When the bishop came on visitation I assumed I would be part of the visitation process, but

Country lady

the parish priest said that he saw no reason for me to be present. After a day's work in the silent presbytery I'd return to my silent, empty house feeling stressed.

Then that same bishop, a man I knew well enough to call by his Christian name, asked me if I would consider being the part time pastoral leader of a country parish up near the NSW border. Its resident priest was needed elsewhere and there was no replacement. This was my cloud walking come to life. I was so delighted that I accepted unquestioningly – didn't talk it over with my spiritual director or spend a few days in prayerful discernment. Just said, yes, when do I go?

It was a three-month-long disaster. None of us had done our homework – neither me nor the bishop nor his advisors. I arrived and was informally introduced to a parish already angry because some years back their children had been sexually abused by a former parish priest. Now they were grieving the loss of their resident priest and further aggrieved at the complete lack of consultation about the future direction of the parish.

I was out of my depth, living four hours away and travelling up for a few days every fortnight, not wanted and trying to put together a much-needed funeral ministry group with parishioners who wanted no part of it. There were secret meetings chaired by a very angry woman, followed by a phone call from someone on the parish council telling me not to return and that they had informed the bishop of their decision.

It was nasty and messy and hurtful. I was angry – with myself, at my own naiveté, with the bishop for putting me in that position, with the people who rejected me. Somewhat bitterly I wondered if my name had been prefixed with Sister this debacle might have turned out differently. Lay women are ready to pick up ministry leadership but not every parishioner is ready for that. Two weeks later, when I

A Gentle Unfolding

returned to collect the few belongings I'd left in the room where I was sleeping, I found them bundled into a cardboard box outside the door.

In the months that followed I tried to pray the tangle of feelings that kept me awake at night. I'd come to a country town carrying my ministry gifts, sure that I had something to offer only to find them not accepted. There was more than a touch of arrogance in this belief of mine and God left me to feel that, to learn from it. I tried to read the signs, to know what to do next.

My father was now in his nineties, still active and living in his own home, but lonely. My daughter, having done the overseas backpack thing, had settled into a relationship. I thought that if I could find a pastoral associate position back in Melbourne I would sell my Waubra house and move back to live with my father. And that's what happened. By the end of 2003 I had resigned from St Alipius', thankfully sold my house for more than I paid for it, put the furniture into storage and moved in with Dad ready to join the Melbourne parish of Our Lady of Perpetual Succour, Maidstone.

There's a verse in chapter 9 of Luke's gospel that I found appropriate the afternoon I packed my car, dropped the keys at the estate agent's office and left Ballarat: 'As for those who do not welcome you, when you leave their town shake the dust from your feet as evidence against them' (Luke 9:5). But it hadn't all been doom and gloom. The cluster of Catholics in Waubra had made me welcome at the fortnightly Masses in the old stone church on the highway opposite my house. I'd met Pauline, a kindred spirit and still a friend. I'd learnt a lot about myself, most of which I found uncomfortable, and I'd discovered that women still had a way to go before they would be seen as co-workers in God's vineyard.

22

Being church in Australia

One crisp Autumn morning in 1840 my great, great grandmother Martha Helyar, her husband Elias and their six children, boarded the sailing ship *Ferguson*, destination Australia. Just over a month later she and one of her year-old twins were buried at sea. We don't really know what happened. There was talk of women and children being mistreated, of an alcoholic doctor, of unexpected storms. What we do know is that four months after leaving Plymouth, only Elias and his remaining five children disembarked on the marshy strip of land known as Port Phillip.

It's the bare bones of a family story, an Australian story, and it's not unusual, because, one way or another, we have all had to cross the sea. Newcomers to Australia today mostly arrive by plane, sometimes coming from countries where the government is oppressive and unjust, countries where peace and justice are no more than words in a dictionary. Along with their suitcases they bring with them a vision of freedom and security for themselves and their families. This yearning to live in peace costs them family, language, food that suits their metabolism, everyday links with their childhood and familiar neighbourhoods.

The first thing I saw when I walked into the church at Maidstone

A Gentle Unfolding

was a massive banner depicting the countries of origin of people in that parish – Vietnam, Ireland, Italy, Croatia, Tonga, Malta, Sudan, Somalia, East Timor, India, Lebanon, Malaysia, Indonesia, New Guinea, the Philippines and Sri Lanka. Framing it were the words of the popular Australian song: 'We are one, but we are many ...' The prophet Ezekiel could have been speaking to us when he said, 'I will take you from the nations and gather you from all the countries and bring you into your own land' (Ezekiel 36:24).

My experience with people outside my own Anglo-Saxon culture had been spasmodic. My father's working life began in the Melbourne market where his father was a leather merchant. After World War II he ran one small business or another in inner Melbourne suburbs where many of his customers were newcomers to Australia. I grew up listening to him telling us some of their stories while we ate our evening meal. Subtly he was teaching me to respect and value the person who is often seen as other.

As a religious woman teaching on an Aboriginal mission, my whitefella superiority was disturbed by one particular young woman about my own age, tall, smiling and so very womanly. Alongside her I felt uncouth and naïve, a perception that grew and eventually led me to leave religious life. Then, in 2002, in a bid to feel useful in a church that didn't seem to have any need for what I had to offer, I spent a month in Bacau, the second largest town in East Timor and a world away from the comfortable settledness of Ballarat where I was still working part time as a pastoral associate.

I thought that I was going to Bacau to help, but what they really needed were carpenters and engineers, bricklayers and electricians, not well-meaning but useless people like me. The people were poor, employment just about non-existent and the electricity supply spasmodic. Many of the houses had been demolished by the Indonesian militia and remained roofless, windowless shells. At the convent where I stayed there was one tap for the community of Timorese sisters and their one hundred boarders. I had arrived in the wet season but the country was experiencing a drought and the creeks and rivers were low if not dry.

The only thing I could do was to live in solidarity with them. I bucketed water for my shower, ate rice with some green vegetable that I never did identify, helped the secondary school boarders with their English homework, did a bit of sewing. In return they gifted me with their days, their laughter, their physical beauty and their faith. They had the kind of faith that got them up early every morning to go to Mass, faith that spoke easily and confidently about their dependence on God, and most of all a faith that enabled them to forgive the terrible things that had happened to their families, their villages, their people. Beside them I felt colourless and insignificant.

With that sobering experience behind me, and because I still needed to earn a living, I was giving the pastoral associate ministry another go. I was now employed to replace a Sister of St Joseph in Maidstone, two parishes sharing the one parish priest, each keeping their individual parish identity. Once again I was joining a pastoral team – two priests, another pastoral associate who looked after the sister parish, and a parish secretary. As with St Christopher's and St Alipius', my responsibilities clustered under an education in faith umbrella.

Over the years, parishes like this one in the western suburbs of Melbourne had been enriched, broadened, sometimes fractured, by the culture and customs of the many differing people who now called Australia home. The practicalities of being church, being Catholic, are much the same wherever one is. No matter how it is dressed up, whatever theological words are used to describe it, the church seems

A Gentle Unfolding

to come across like any other institution, with buildings, financial parameters, authority structures and lots of staff.

One of my first tasks in the Maidstone parish was to coordinate a small group to reflect on the Lenten gospels This evolved into a prayer group that met weekly. There were ten of us, predominantly women, born in ten different countries. Somehow it worked, despite our inherited prayer practices and differing images of God. The gospels, the basis of our prayer and reflection, speak a universal language.

When any institution is two thousand years old it's bound to get bogged down in pre-packaged formulas, doctrines and organisational practicalities, especially under a hierarchical male leadership. It's not surprising that generations of religious practices take precedence in the spiritual lives of people who feel disenfranchised by a church that seemingly has a love affair with words and correct ideas, when all people yearn for are ways to make religion real and relevant in their everyday.

For that to happen in a new country you need language. For a time I coordinated a group of women who gathered for a weekly English lesson. I use the term loosely because although they called me teacher it was really a women's club. We talked about everything – in English – and even went for a train ride into the centre of Melbourne! Most of the group were Vietnamese, one or two were Sudanese; there was also a woman who had emigrated from Italy thirty years earlier and a visiting Indonesian woman who wanted some English so she could talk to her Australian grandchildren. Some were Catholic, some were Buddhist, but the barriers were non-existent as we shared the ups and downs of our lives. It was a wonderfully energising experience for me, and I thank them for it.

As time passes, old religious customs and perceptions tend to lose their meaning in a new country and a different environment. The

Being church in Australia

early settlers in Australia had brought with them a strongly Irish Catholic faith, an approach that remained dominant for the next hundred years. In primary school I was enthralled by stories about these first Australian Catholics, lay people, who managed to keep their faith alive for the thirty years before Catholic chaplains were permitted in the colony. In the absence of Mass they gathered to pray the rosary, a practice— like building schools and hospitals — that became a distinguishing mark of the 'good Catholic'.

After World War II came immigration. Along with pasta, wine and real coffee, the European newcomers brought with them religious practices that were more emotive, very different to the prevailing Irish heritage. Vatican II followed about the same time as another influx of migrants, this time from Asia, the Philippines and South America. Along with the delights of Asian food we were introduced to new parishioners who clung fiercely to the faith of their fathers and mothers and knew what it was like to be persecuted for it.

Meaningful liturgy is a challenge in parishes where parishioners have different ways of expressing faith and spirituality. I vacillated between religious-type acceptance and full-blown frustration when a Filipino choir persuaded the parish priest to let them sing at the Sunday night Mass. The liturgical purist in me objected to the dicey theology and childish words of most of the hymns they chose. When I was told it was the custom on Holy Thursday for twelve Italian men, dressed in apostle-style robes, to stand behind the celebrant during the Mass before having their feet washed, I stood my liturgical ground and the parish priest's deep desire for a peaceful life and insisted that instead we approached women and men more representative of the parish diversity.

The first year this happened it didn't go down well, or the second year either. But by end of the third year a more diverse group

A Gentle Unfolding

of women and men was seen as an inclusive way to celebrate Holy Thursday liturgy in our multi-cultural parish. The Vietnamese liked to celebrate their national day with a Mass, reflective and reverent, and a noisy dragon which wasn't and which drew the unfavourable attention of the diocesan hierarchy.

Theological reflection on practices such as religious processions, dragons and statues with little artistic merit but a lot of glitter can help retain the deep Christian truths each holds, and may suggest new ways of expressing them. This will take time and courage, but out of it will come a uniquely Australian way of celebrating our Catholic faith.

We are a young nation and our Australian way of being church is still young. Just as the gum tree sheds its bark, some loved customs and words will drop away. However, if we look closely at the smooth white trunk that the stripped bark has exposed, we will notice tiny new shoots. That's us, growing and nurturing the church of the future, strong and vibrant, a rich mix of Asian, European and Aboriginal cultures.

When Pope John Paul II was in Alice Springs in 1986 he said: 'The church in Australia will not be fully the church that Jesus wants her to be until you have made your contribution to her life, and until that contribution has been joyfully received by others.' He was talking to the Aboriginal people but his words could equally apply to the mix of nationalities that are currently in the process of becoming Australians.

During my three years at Maidstone, my father died, Mary-jane married and my youngest brother and I pooled our financial resources and furniture and bought a house that suited our differing needs. Working in such a large parish, balancing the challenges continually thrown up by its multicultural character, being expected to attend all the weekend Masses including Saturday and Sunday evening, coupled with my increasing age, began to tire me out.

Being church in Australia

I decided that my pastoral associate days were coming to an end. The catalyst when it came was all but hidden, but a turning point nevertheless. For close on forty years I had prepared children for first communion. For all of those years I had struggled with the church's ruling that required eight-year-olds to receive the sacrament of reconciliation before making their first communion. Now, no matter how creatively I had become at packaging preparation for reconciliation, how few times I used the word sin, I just couldn't face telling yet another group of little kids that they were sinners years before they had figured out the ins and outs of relating to others. At the end of 2006 I handed in my resignation and officially retired.

23
All beginnings have endings

Australian writer David Malouf, in his book *An Imaginary Life*, says it so well: 'What else should our lives be but a series of beginnings, of painful settings out into the unknown, pushing off from the edges of consciousness into the mystery of what we have not yet become?' The beginning of 2007 was my new beginning, and there was nothing imaginary about it.

The Maidstone parish had farewelled me with a morning tea on my last Sunday as a pastoral associate. While change and I get on well together, I'm not very good with farewells, a hangover from religious life when leaving anywhere was a serious matter involving obedience and avoiding anything to do with an 'unhealthy' attachment to people or places. So, as I smiled my way through my formal goodbyes, I let the flattering words slide away and did my best to duck the sneaky feeling of loss that was beginning to make itself felt. The parish priest proudly presented me with a large box, which turned out to contain a Sunbeam Mixmaster. I was aware that I can be a stirrer, but – a mixer? Thankfully the parish secretary whispered that she had the receipt, so sneakily I took it back and replaced it with a silver bracelet.

And so ended another segment of my life. I'd been so busy for so long, so impatient and frustrated with the institutional church, that

All beginnings have endings

I'd begun to lose touch with the deeper dimensions of the ordinary. Retirement was a gift, a time to slow down and take pleasure in my home and my family. St John of the Cross said God's words to us are written inside ordinary experiences. Closer to our own time Thomas Merton followed it up when, over and over again, he said that our real self, the one that God knows, is to be found in the context of our daily realities. Well, in retirement my daily realities would be very ordinary indeed.

I put the alarm clock in a drawer, cleaned the kitchen cupboards and sorted out practicalities like superannuation. Working within the Catholic Church will never make you rich, so I had no trouble qualifying for a government pension. Back in the early 1990s when lay pastoral associates like me were the exception, parishes had only budgeted for the stipend usually paid to religious women. As the number of lay pastoral associates grew they became more outspoken about an institution that preached justice but in practice was often an unjust employer. My first parish priest employer was a younger man, a little more in tune with financial realities, who offered me a wage that, while less than that paid to Catholic school teachers, was acceptable, accompanied as it was with the use of a car and a petrol card. Unfortunately it would be seven years before that wage was increased.

Guilt, that thing with a long tail that Catholics of my generation can't seem to shake off, often shadowed my need for a slightly bigger salary. I knew that the money had to come from somewhere and that place seemed to be the pockets of the parishioners, not the rather better-off institutional church. Over the years, wages and conditions for church employees have improved. Even though what was clearly an injustice has been righted, an unspoken assumption still lingers that working for the church is a personal privilege and one did so, if not voluntarily, then at a reduced rate of pay.

A Gentle Unfolding

All the years of my working life had been centred on church. I had defined who I was by how I was named and what I did. I left behind my family name and the name my parents had chosen for me at birth and became known as Sister Mary Andrina. Twenty years later, back in civvies, I adjusted quickly to being known as Miss Scully, working first as a primary teacher then on a catechist team. I replaced my religious vows with those of marriage and became Terry's wife, Mrs Lynch. Our foster family of children came to us through a church agency and in the absence of their birth mother they called me Mum. I taught in Catholic schools where the pupils invariably called me Miss. As a pastoral associate I liked both adults and children to call me Judith, my given name. Now who was I?

Sixteen years as a pastoral associate had left that dragon woman inside me curled up in a cave, fire damped down, overcome by the Saint Georges outside. With retirement I was conscious of a feeling of anticipation accompanied by the flutter of fear that comes with a new beginning. There was much in parish ministry that gave me satisfaction. I liked being part of a team, I liked working with women and men with whom I shared a common interest and focus. I appreciated the freedom to design programs that met parish needs. I enjoyed introducing children to the Jesus of the gospels. It was flattering to consider myself as giving the church a female face. But that wasn't enough. It didn't matter what theological words were used to describe the pastoral associate ministry, people like me ended up being referred to as 'Father's helper'.

When someone died, most families expected to see the priest, not the pastoral associate. When families felt the need of counselling, they rang the presbytery doorbell and asked to see the priest, even though his priestly training didn't automatically qualify him to deal with issues peculiar to marriage and family life. In only one of the

All beginnings have endings

three parishes where I have worked was marriage preparation given by a team of married couples. I've been to funerals in many different parishes where the liturgy was perfunctory and impersonal. I've witnessed baptisms where the physical symbols and actions were swallowed up in church-speak. These priests were good men, but tired and overwhelmed by the magnitude of what was expected of them by people and canon law.

The bishops of Australia came up with a couple of solutions that were in line with the expectations of the institutional church. They imported priests from other parts of the world to fill the gaps in parishes across Australia. These priests had the energy that comes with youth, but they came from more needy parts of the world and brought with them very different expectations of being church. I found them difficult to work with and I'm sure that they had a problem fitting in with women like me, women who didn't seem to understand their place in church or society.

Sunday after Sunday, one priest in particular whose accent was so difficult to follow that the sermon he preached – and it was a sermon, not a homily – was largely unintelligible. As a pastoral associate doing my Sunday duty, I sat through each of his Masses and blew a little dragon smoke about the injustice of it all. As an ordained male he was permitted to open up the Word of God, whether we understood him or not. I wasn't.

Vatican II, now receding into the background of church thinking and policy, had encouraged me to believe that God's gift of priestly ministry was not limited by gender, that women and men could spread the good news of Gospel as equals. I knew without a doubt that God gifted some women with a vocation to the priesthood. But I knew too that the invitation, while not withdrawn, could not be accepted in my lifetime. Once I would have settled for being a deacon as a step along

A Gentle Unfolding

the way. Now I see the two ministries as two different callings. My dragon woman, who had longed to uncurl, to swish her tail and flex her wings, bit by bit was losing some of her fire.

Maria, my pastoral associate partner at St Christopher's and like me a mum with children, was more than a work colleague. She had an openness about her that I valued but didn't always find in other pastoral associates. I found her support invaluable. Also at St Christopher's was Pat, secretary par excellence, who, in the days before I became computer literate, cheerfully typed the many bits and pieces of my ripples sheets. Mostly, though, parish secretaries I encountered seemed happiest with a pyramid model of church with pastoral associates occupying the bottom line. They were polite and helpful, but didn't like the way I treated priests as colleagues. I guess they thought it lacked the respect that was owed to the priesthood. I believe that respect has to be earned. Nevertheless, with one or two exceptions I have unreserved respect and more, for the priests with whom I shared ministry.

Now all that was over. I was retired and the structure that had cupped me for all those years was now a dotted line under my religious practice and beliefs. God had called and I had followed, one step after another, always living and working within the parameters of church. For years the institution that is the Catholic Church had frustrated me even as it connected me to the God of my baptism. While the basics of my childhood faith hadn't changed, how I understood them and lived them had. I had come to question and challenge beliefs and practices, traditions, papal declarations, rules and hearsay that are held dear by many Catholics.

I believed that the most pressing question facing the church concerned the priesthood, not the role of women or families. I struggled with outdated rubrics and ecclesiastical clothing that belonged to

All beginnings have endings

another time. I questioned the value of Catholic schools at the expense of aged care and housing for refugees and the homeless. I wondered why every parish didn't offer spiritual direction and pastoral counselling as a ministry.

As a pastoral associate, my role in the church had been 'to assist the parish priest in leading the mission and pastoral care of the parish community in accordance with the precepts, teachings and practices of the Catholic Church'. Put like that, my freedom to live and speak the full truth, as I saw it, was limited. Other women were coming behind me, younger and better equipped to be the face of the church of the future.

Much of my pastoral ministry had been focused on helping others to recognise God in the ordinary of life. It's one thing to preach it, another to live it. When Jesus comes knocking – 'Behold I stand at the door and knock' – it would no longer be a presbytery door but the door to the home I shared with my youngest brother. It was up to me to open it and invite God to share the uneventful and the commonplace that would characterise my future life.

24
Once upon a story

Maybe I'm a bit of a word junkie because I was conceived in the residence behind my parent's first business, a suburban bookshop and lending library. Or maybe it's my dad's influence – his insistence that words be used correctly – or my childhood weekly visit to the municipal library for stories by Enid Blyton and May Gibbs, moving on to Mary Grant Bruce and Ethel Turner. When I outgrew these in my early teens, I read books left over from that early bookshop library, devouring them with little or no understanding of their adult context, but a subconscious appreciation of their structure and vocabulary.

Then it all stopped. The only books available to young religious like me were lives of the saints, accounts of Marian apparitions and spiritual theology written in the dense language favoured by the religious academics of the day. I hungered for fiction. Much to my slightly guilty delight my first mission convent had a collection of Agatha Christie whodunits and Georgette Heyer fairyfloss paperbacks. My literary drought was over and even if my intellect was still starved my imagination said thank you as I read my way through the compulsory midday siesta.

Op shops and weekend markets with their once-upon-time

Once upon a story

treasures and long forgotten must-haves draw me. But it's the second-hand books that are my big attraction. I usually go home with two or three tempting titles by forgotten authors and a crick in my neck from trying to read book titles sideways. Books spill out of my bookshelves, hide in the bedside cabinet, jostle for space on the coffee table and pile up on my work table.

Reading informative articles online extends my mind and broadens my knowledge base and I load modern fiction on to my Kindle for relaxation reading. I read poetry for the joy of words that flow like rippled silk and I dip delightedly into journals that surprise me with our shared uniqueness.

I read theology slowly, with a highlighter in my hand, savouring it in small bites, giving it time to connect with the scripture that underpins my faith and the dailyness that grounds me. When Joseph Campbell, the great scholar of myths, asked what spiritual practice he followed, he replied, 'I underline books.' Me too!

I spend an inordinate amount of time – and money – in the children's section of bookshops, marvelling at the artwork and ingenuity of story books ostensibly written for children. In the intellectual world of church there's something vaguely not-grown-up about confessing that I am nourished spiritually by the mystical quality of children's picture story books, as they reach long symbolic fingers into desires and yearnings that defy words.

I don't recall exactly when the reading began to spill over into writing. As a young teen I won a municipal competition with an essay about a character called Thomas Bent, but after that nothing. Maybe Siloam was the catalyst. As well as being a turning point in my life and spirituality it required me to write regular essays, and while I didn't exactly enjoy the time that entailed I discovered the joy of stringing words together, having them say what I meant and at the same time

A Gentle Unfolding

opening me up to a deeper understanding of what lay beneath them. The only drawback to this kind of writing was my inability to type. I persuaded my fifteen-year-old daughter to type my Siloam assignments. The truth was, I was scared of the computer, assumed it was beyond my competence.

Terry's death left me with space to fill and the energy to try something new. I bought a computer and did one of those beginner's courses that libraries run to help IT novices like me. Very quickly my machine and I became inseparable, a relationship frequently frustrated by my incompetence. A few years later I had one of those birthdays that end in a nought and my computer savvy youngest brother gave me a gift right out of left field. He offered to set me up with my own website. Thus the Tarella Spirituality website came into being. I began writing a weekly gospel reflection and posting it to a few interested people.

For two thousand years, excluding the century after Jesus' death, Catholic women had been excluded from preaching the Word of God in a public setting. This not only saddened me but irritated me, because for all those centuries, Sunday after Sunday, the Good News has been skewered to male terminology and experience.

Twenty years ago, lectures by scripture scholar Sister Shelia Byrne rsm had given me the tools to better understand the Bible and the confidence to bring my feminine perspective to what I read. Gradually I learnt to trust my own peculiarly feminine experience of God and how I lived out that relationship. I wanted to open up the Word of God from a female perspective and to share that with others.

At the same time I was aware of a reluctance to speak out from a feminine viewpoint, even though my life as a Catholic woman had involved me in many different facets of church life. It would mean signing my name under what I wrote, owning the words as mine. I

Once upon a story

was neither a theologian nor an academic. What right had I to slot the Jesus story into words around the ordinary of my life?

I'd spent almost a lifetime with a long list of Catholic 'no-go' areas – restrictions, rules and unchallenged traditions. Now I was turning my back on an authoritarian male leadership structure to interpret the Sunday gospel in a way they might judge to be inappropriate for such a sacred task. It would be much easier to settle for something safe – like a feel-good blog. But my time of always being spoken for by a patriarchy was over. Under the web banner Tarella Spirituality – *finding God in the everyday* – I wrote my first gospel reflection and pressed send.

I called that first reflection, and the ones that followed, Connexions – connecting your story with the Jesus story. But God words don't touch our hearts unless they come wrapped in personal experience. In tarellaspirituality.com I wrote words that I hoped were theologically sound and scripturally based but without the church-speak. Jesus the storyteller talked about the things that made up the everyday of his life – a single candle lighting up a hillside, a dab of yeast in a bowl of flour, a pinch of salt flavouring a dish, a seed that holds the whole of life. I wrote as a woman, a wife, a mother, and with all the intimacies and experiences that go with that.

Religious institutions are good at organising, but they don't always have the language, or even the freedom of expression, that touches into our God-hunger. Institutional religion doesn't understand the ordinary way most of us live our lives and they pad out their understanding in words, words that end up meaning very little to the average household. Up until Vatican II, most spiritual books were written from the perspective and lifestyle of religious, men and women, but mostly male. In the fifty years since then, women have been finding their voice and their niche, but the fact is books about Christian

A Gentle Unfolding

spirituality don't sell very well. And websites like mine are no match for Facebook or celebrity blogs.

I'm not good at putting words around a subject face to face. I am only myself when the words start to shape themselves in my journal or on my laptop. I write to find out what I'm thinking, to get beneath something, turn it upside down, shake it and see what words drop out. I touch into any unease that I feel, discover new directions for my longing. That's one of the ways God and I communicate. God shows me what's been there all the time.

Like everybody else, I absorb and integrate insights from a broad range of sources – conversations, newspapers, the internet, books, world events, family, film, song. When it comes to shaping them into connections and images that relate to the ordinary of life and the inner pull of God, I usually end up sitting in front of a blank screen with nothing to write. I just have to wait, to sink into my inner self where God dwells.

What surfaces is usually something subtle, obscure, personal, something I might find hard to express, a topic that needs a beginning as well as a middle and an end, not just a whisper of an idea. I pick it up, turn it over and usually sigh. Words like affirm, inspire, challenge, change, disturb, come to mind. Then God takes pity on me and I start making notes and the sun comes out. This is writing as prayer. As Jeremiah so poetically put it, 'Then Yahweh put out his hand and touched my mouth and said to me, "There, I am putting words into your mouth"' (Jeremiah 1:9).

The belief that I have something to say keeps me posting pieces on my website. Most of my readers are women who long for the kind of spiritual nourishment that picks up where religious education classes or Sunday school left off and liturgy or homilies fail to pick up. I use language that feels at home in a coffee shop or around the kitchen

Once upon a story

table, always adult, and varied enough to 'touch a spot', topics that value women's gifts and differentness. I want my words and images to be recognisably Australian, the kind that tap into the inner spaces that are so much part of being Australian.

Occasionally, I submit something to one of the Australian catholic internet sites or magazines. CathNews, a website under the auspices of the Catholic bishops of Australia, used to have a column called Cathblog, a forum where writers could voice a Christian dimension to differing aspects of religion and spirituality. I appreciate responses because writing the way I do is like sharing something personal with another and trusting that someone out there is reading and listening to what I have to say. It has been an eye-opener to discover that responses can vary from appreciative and affirming to demeaning, offensive and occasionally abusive.

So what keeps me writing? It's a need. Jeremiah says it so well: 'I say to myself, I will not mention God, I will speak God's name no more. But then it becomes like fire burning in my heart, imprisoned in my bones. I grow weary holding it in. I cannot endure it.' His words take me back to my sixteen-year-old self, in love with God even though I have no idea why or where it will take me. Love is all the things Paul said it was, and it's a fire in the belly too. Writing is my late life answer to God's original call. That call has led me through religious life, teaching, marriage, mothering and pastoral ministry, and all the time the fire has never quite gone out.

25
One size fits all

'I have never felt comfortable praying. I almost feel I should put the word in quotes, as I'm never quite sure that what I do deserves the name.' When I read these words of faith writer and poet Christian Wiman, I felt a wave of something akin to relief. I've always found prayer to be undefinable, and here was someone putting words around it for me.

The way I learnt to pray came out of the Catholic tradition – morning offering and night prayers; the go-to standbys of the Our Father and the Hail Mary linked together in the rosary; novenas – nine days of please-please-please requests to Mary or a saint highly recommended for specialised kinds of need – and prayer books full of words considered suitable to address God in a multitude of different situations.

Religious life introduced me to a modified version of the priest's Office accompanied by daily Mass and meditation, and devotions peculiar to the Daughters of Our Lady of the Sacred Heart. Added to this was thirty minutes of personal prayer that I was expected to fit in to an already crowded day. I ended up with spiritual indigestion.

In the convent I read book after book about prayer written by people whose religious lifestyle was also their profession. Some were

One size fits all

technical, focused on moving from one level of prayer to another, higher, level, like some kind of ladder to God. As a married woman I hoped that the words and insights of those vaguely remembered books could give me a one-size-fits-all recipe for prayer. But they contained descriptions of prayer that was never interrupted by toddler or teenage tantrums, dropping children at sporting events or the necessity to have dinner on the table, boredom and sleepiness.

Teresa of Avila had come highly recommended, but she lost me when she talked about how to handle God's special favours. I'd had none of those. There was the other Therese, the one known as the Littler Flower, and while I appreciated her emphasis on the ordinary, her words and life experience didn't touch my inner need. It wasn't until years later, reading a novel where one of the characters was described as having an itch in his heart, that I realised that's what I had, a God itch, a God need — and I hadn't known what to do about it.

When I left religious life, along with my veil I shed the one-size-fits-all of monastic prayer and the mix of devotional practices that accompanied it, and I never pined for any of them. I confined my formal prayer to Sunday Mass. Anything else was on the run — parking spots, a child home late, a sick friend. But, subtly, God began reminding me that the discipline of religious techniques, formulas, practices and places that I had been led to believe defined prayer were just its foundation. Life itself was the prayer, the tensions and joys, disappointments and timelines, struggles and breakthroughs that I experienced and the way they swirled around inside me. God and I experienced them together.

When I hear someone say that they are spiritual but not religious I mentally translate it as, 'I have a space inside me that is God-shaped and I don't know quite how to fill it.' Spirituality makes real what religion talks about. That yearning, undefinable space that is inside

A Gentle Unfolding

each of us is prayer-shaped. Who I am is how I pray – and so I pray as a woman.

My life spirals and circles in and around family and friends. Relationships are intertwined with my female DNA. Over the years I've had a household to run and employers to satisfy, interspersed with all manner of relationships that have both enriched and challenged me. Sometimes in the chaos of it all my God relationship felt non-existent, more often it was a mish-mash of on-the-run practices and approaches. So when I say that prayer is the way I express my relationship with the mystery I call God, then I am saying that the ups and downs and roundabouts that marked the ordinary of my days were, and are, the stuff of that prayer.

Women are relational and when they get together they talk about connection and brokenness, about love and work, about experiences of powerlessness and vulnerability. Their words never move in a straight line. Backward and forward they go, now repeating themselves before moving on with another connection, then returning to the beginning. To a listening male it can seem disconnected, fragmented and repetitive, never going anywhere. But it's always about the ever-changing dimensions of relationship.

Men's talk seems to go in straight lines or step by step, like a ladder. The overwhelmingly male institutional church is no different. Western Christianity and the way it is lived is intimately tied up with language, verbal expression, sermons, creeds, catechism and theology – all very cerebral. Following Vatican II, women, overwhelmingly women with a religious life background, not only replaced their medieval clothing for something more appropriate but began writing books about prayer and spirituality. They explored scripture with a woman's eye and wrote about the way it touched into their own story. Their words assured me that the deep emotional, sexual and psycho-

One size fits all

logical needs that underpinned my individuality were not something considered suspect in God's eyes, but a gift.

I had never been very good at talking about God as a loving reality in my life. It was only as I read what this new wave of spiritual writers had to say that I gradually began to trust my feel-good approach to God. I'd find myself musing about the God I was brought up to believe was the all-seeing, all-knowing recipient of prayer and scholarly words, not for moments of quiet musing. As a small child I remember trying to solve the mystery that was God. I decided that if I thought back far enough maybe I could reach God's beginnings. Religion class had introduced me to the words 'for ever … and ever … and ever …', so I tried that, reaching out into an immeasurable and unimaginable past and future. God is mystery and the response to mystery is faith.

The way women experience faith is more likely to be embodied than expressed verbally. When a woman is freed to let go of her childhood image of God, with its parental and authoritarian overtones, it is likely to be replaced by something tactile, embodying qualities and experiences deeper than their shape, colour, sound, smell, texture or taste. A young woman told me once that she felt she touched God the creator at the birth of her child. I have found God in the vast red plains of Central Australia and among the skinny gum trees that I see from the window of the room where I write. I have sensed God in the smell of freshly baked bread and in the healing touch of my chiropractor.

Naming God is tricky. My God cannot be confined to the masculinity current in church liturgies, but neither can I bring myself to call God She. Holy One does nothing for me, nor does Goddess – although I once wrote a piece about my feminine need for a God image under the heading 'A high-heeled image of God'.

I feel comfortable naming God as Sophia. Passages from Ecclesi-

A Gentle Unfolding

astes, Proverbs, Baruch and Wisdom have been passed over when it comes to Sunday liturgies and scripture study. Yet these are the books in the Bible where God is named Sophia, the Greek for wisdom. In poetic language, God is manifested as female, giving direction to life and intimately bonded in God's creative presence. Sophia is pictured as light, as the breath of God, as a woman sitting by the city gate, and, delightfully, as a child at play.

To address God as Sophia is to move beyond the words and images that call to mind the power, strength and assertiveness of a male world. For women like me who have tired of God images that don't recognise their empathy, creativity and relational gifts, Sophia comes with the breath of new life.

When I approach the mystery that is God using Sophia imagery it gives me the freedom to do so as a woman. Wisdom implies roundness: the sort of wholeness that comes from experience and inwardly integrating that experience, seeing the connections, gradually moving the endless walls and screens we put up to hide us from God.

I have met many prayerful women who no longer feel nourished by the institutional church. They might look like the women you see at the supermarket, at a daytime movie, having a coffee mid-morning or catching a bus – maybe retired, often over the first flush of life and occasionally into the next stage as well. They can talk family, cooking, gardening, politics and their faith with varying degrees of insight and fluidity, but there's more to them than that. I call them Sophia women.

Every month or so for some years I met with some of these Sophia women. We talked about what was going on in our lives. It was mostly ordinary stuff with an extra-ordinary edge. Almost without noticing it, their God relationship deepened as they learnt to recognise the subtle voice and movements of the Spirit in the constant to and fro

One size fits all

of their common storytelling. In church-speak it's called theological reflection.

Sophia women are serious about their spirituality. Mostly alone, though sometimes as part of a group, they work hard to nurture their God relationship. While some meditate regularly, others journal or read books by people like Richard Rohr or Joan Chittester. And, without exception, all of them live with a creative openness to the needs of others, whether it's family, friends or the wider community.

There is something about Sophia women that looks and feels like freedom. Their attention to God's voice as they hear it, their acceptance of life as it unfolds, has set them free to recognise their inner truth and wisdom, to give it voice. They've weathered toddler meltdowns, teenage rebellion, money shortages, unfulfilling jobs, relationship hiccups and worse. Their people skills are formidable. They have learnt that not everyone sees the world the same way and it has led them to create strategies that open the way to ongoing and loving communication. Many have moved beyond the boundaries of traditional ways of being church, because they offer them no valid outlet for their female giftedness.

Like all of us, I was born with a hunger for God. The intensity of that hunger was gradually overlaid by the needs of marriage, family and earning a living. Then, as the grey crept into my hair and our children grew up and left home, God activated that old itch in my heart. I learnt that adult prayer can be compared to mature adult love. It's about sitting in companionable silence with someone we love, hearing what is unspoken, finishing one another's sentences, finding that there is still the possibility of being surprised.

The prayer invitation of late middle age and beyond is to let go of the wordy and formal prayers of younger years, to stop the endless chatter in our heads and let some silence in. Silence is challenging. I

A Gentle Unfolding

know. I create all kinds of distractions and noise in my life to avoid it, to escape it. Way back in the 1300s Meister Eckhart said that nothing resembles the language of God as much as silence does. I have a recurring memory of my grandson Harry, home after a long day in childcare, patting the sofa and saying to his father, 'Sit here.' There were no more words, just the closeness with his dad. Was this the way Jesus prayed to his Father?

The things we label as silence, such as an early morning or late night solitary sup of tea, a long soaking bath, enjoying the roar of the surf or the carol of a magpie, can be prayer and a time to hear the still, quiet voice of God. It's called contemplative prayer. Contemplative prayer doesn't see life as a division between religious stuff and everything else. It looks below the surface and deepens the way we see ordinary things, something theologian Karl Rahner called 'the mysticism of ordinary life'.

It takes faith, and practice, to recognise the voice of God in something as ordinary as the words of a song or the smile of a stranger. For what might be only a moment we have a glimpse of something beyond, and it leaves us with a message of peace wrapped in a shaft of joy.

26

You can't lose the plot

In late 2012 I decided that a sabbatical type experience might enable me to hear the core message of the Gospel in new, relevant and creative ways, to regain whatever was missing in my life. Maybe time spent in the company of those I considered to be peers or role-models would rev up my flagging enthusiasm for things religious.

After reading lots of online brochures from all parts of the USA, Canada, Ireland and England, and careful examination of my finances, I chose a Redemptorist-led three month renewal program for women and men in pastoral ministry, to be held in the depths of the British countryside.

In Autumn 2013, after the long flight from Australia, I touched down in the UK, full of excited anticipation and unaware that in the group of twenty-three, twenty were either priests or nuns. There were missionaries with years of ministry behind them, a few teaching nuns on sabbatical and a high proportion from parts of the world where Catholicism was fairly recent, where religious women were set apart, below the priest but above their married sisters and cousins. I was the only married person.

The structured program and the fussy rules and regulations that

A Gentle Unfolding

we were expected to follow had echoes of my novitiate days. My formation in religious life followed by years of church ministry and further education had given me a good basic knowledge of scripture and theology and I was familiar with church-speak, but when I didn't turn up to all the formal prayer opportunities that punctuated the week. my sabbatical companions weren't sure what to make of me. I felt very secular and worldly and somehow inferior to these women and men who had remained faithful to their vocation and whose piety was admirable.

There were things I loved – the thrill of living in a three hundred-year-old heritage-listed Georgian mansion, Saturday bus trips to tourist destinations that were a cross between history and familiar fiction, lecturers who knew their topics and presented them well. There was a mid-term break when the majority of participants went on pilgrimage to the Holy Land or Iona – while I spent a wonderful few days in Paris.

I would leave a lecture fired up by the presenter's words, wanting to hear how others had heard them, keen to explore the possibilities the topics offered for personal spirituality and the widespread ministries of the group. But it never happened. I had crossed the world with the expectation that my flagging spirit would be renewed, unaware that such renewal is slow, coming in God's good time.

My sabbatical space was visually beautiful, but instead of the renewal of spirit that I had expected, I felt ignored and devalued, an ex-religious and a second-rate Catholic. I was way out of my comfort zone during those three months, revisiting the choices I had made and the way I was living out my vocation.

Eighteen months later, back home, I was invited to attend the biannual Australian Catholic Communications Congress. The majority of participants were lay people, mostly women. They were vibrant and often downright sassy and in them I caught a glimpse of the

You can't lose the plot

woman I had been decades before – enthusiastic and committed to using my giftedness in the service of the Body of Christ. My sabbatical experience had left me doubting the value of my years of ministry, now I had an overwhelming sense that the women and men I met at that congress were walking in my footsteps and those of others like me, that the Good News was in safe hands. Only now was I able to freely accept that my years of religious life were, and are, part of God's plot, my true self. They're stuck to me, and that's OK.

In the more than fifty years since the last Vatican II document was printed and distributed, I had never quite lost the energy, the buzz, the breath of the Spirit that has kept my passion for the things of God alive – or the embarrassment that can accompany it. Michael Leunig, the social commentator and cartoonist, once said, 'You can't lose the plot. It's stuck to you.' While a passion for a football team is seen as normal, it's more acceptable to settle for passivity when it comes to something as counter-cultural as religion. God is distinctly personal and private, for praying, for deep reflection and scholarly words.

My in-love-with-God fifteen-year-old self had only a vague awareness of the cost of love. As the prophet Jeremiah said when he described his relationship with God, 'God has seduced me …' (Jeremiah 20:7). No wonder it's said we fall in love. If I had known the depths of that fall I would never have been brave enough to leave home. I let myself be seduced and the seduction has wound its way through a life of joys and losses – of aloneness too. I sometimes felt that God was a jealous lover.

Passion is like fire whose shape cannot be limited or contained. It's free-form, dancing, leaping, crackling, enthralling, eye-catching. It's only in hindsight that you recognise how it has danced you into unexpected twists and turnings. It asks question and pushes boundaries.

In retirement, I felt free to move beyond the boundaries imposed

A Gentle Unfolding

by formal church ministry, to ask questions that formerly I had suppressed as being disloyal. Away from the centre where orthodoxy resided I could disagree with a papal remark which assured the faithful that claiming a priestly vocation is merely personal attraction when the person is female. I could not accept that bishops were the right persons to make far-reaching and definitive decisions about family matters or forbid grieving people to insert appropriate personal touches into funeral liturgies.

When I needed support and encouragement I found it in books written by women who had overcome institutional obstacles and resentment to become theologians and scripture scholars. Every time I pushed yet another boundary, questioning beliefs that authority figures in our institutional church consider sacred and immovable, or challenged yet one more so-called traditional practice, I did it knowing that I wasn't the first to do so.

As Vatican II faded into the past, conservative elements in the church pushed for tighter controls on liturgy and moral issues. Like the two friends trudging along the road to Emmaus, I had expectations. 'I had hoped' that in my lifetime women would gradually take their place alongside men, baptising babies, anointing the sick to whom they took communion, bringing a feminine perspective to the Sunday homilies. It hadn't happened and it didn't look like it was going to become church practice any time soon.

The expression 'softly prophetic' sums up the women and men like me who once were criticised for 'losing their vocation'. Not so! We carried the gifts of religious life into lay ministry and pointed the way to a whole new generation of discipleship, often ministering outside the ecclesiastical net and bringing something new and vibrant into the church.

As a Daughter of Our Lady of the Sacred Heart I wore an oval-

You can't lose the plot

shaped image of Mary around my neck. These days I wear a gum nut dipped in silver. Jesus' image of a seed has been a constant in my life. The magnificent ghost gum outside the window where I write was once a dream inside its mother gum nut. A long-ago fire split it open, releasing the life inside. Now, year after year, strip by tattered strip, the tree it grew into sheds its old skin and bares new smooth, creamy bark beneath.

Gum trees keep me grounded. They tell me that I have to let go of the past to make way for the future. They remind me that fire is the catalyst that splits the gum nut, that I am a disciple of the man who said he came to cast fire on the earth

The fifteen-year-old I once was would need to let the fire do its work when she fell in love with God and called it a vocation. Like the life within the seed, my vocation held a call from God that would lead me into new places, new ways of doing and being. I have become a seed planter, dreaming dreams and enkindling the fire that will warm tomorrow's church.

Judith Scully, a fourth generation Australian, was a toddler when World War II began. A lifetime later her memorabilia box overflows with bits and pieces from her years as a religious sister teaching on Aboriginal settlements, marriage, parenting five children, three of them fostered and two adopted, running a general store, the untimely death of her husband from motor neurone disease, and nearly two decades as a pastoral associate in Catholic parishes. That experience fuelled her passion to affirm the way women live out their spirituality in the ordinariness of everyday.

In retirement Judith re-discovered her love of words and these days reaches out to women at her website, Words from the Edge – www.judithscully.com.au. She and her youngest brother share a home among the gum trees in Warrandyte, Victoria.

www.ingramcontent.com/pod-product-compliance
Lightning Source LLC
Chambersburg PA
CBHW021108080526
44587CB00010B/443